Object-oriented Languages

Basic principles and programming techniques

Michel Beaudouin-Lafon

Université de Paris-Sud
Translated by Jack Howlett

CHAPMAN & HALL

London · Glasgow · Weinheim · New York · Tokyo · Melbourne · Madras

Published by Chapman & Hall, 2–6 Boundary Row, London SE1 8HN, UK

Chapman & Hall, 2–6 Boundary Row, London SE1 8HN, UK

Blackie Academic & Professional, Wester Cleddens Road, Bishopbriggs, Glasgow G64 2NZ, UK

Chapman & Hall GmbH, Pappelallee 3, 69469 Weinheim, Germany

Chapman & Hall Inc., One Penn Plaza, 41st Floor, New York NY 10119, USA

Chapman & Hall Japan, Thomson Publishing Japan, Hirakawacho Nemoto Building, 6F, 1-7-11 Hirakawa-cho, Chiyoda-ku, Tokyo 102, Japan

Chapman & Hall Australia, Thomas Nelson Australia, 102 Dodds Street, South Melbourne, Victoria 3205, Australia

Chapman & Hall India, R. Seshadri, 32 Second Main Road, CIT East, Madras 600 035, India

First English Language edition 1994

© 1994 Chapman & Hall

Original French language edition – Les Langages à Objets – 1992, Armand Colin Éditeur.

Typeset in 10/12 Palatino by EXPO Holdings, Malaysia
Printed in Great Britain by St Edmundsbury Press, Bury St Edmunds

ISBN 0 412 55800 9

A catalogue record for this book is available from the British Library

Library of Congress Catalog Card Number: 93-74885

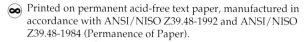 Printed on permanent acid-free text paper, manufactured in accordance with ANSI/NISO Z39.48-1992 and ANSI/NISO Z39.48-1984 (Permanence of Paper).

Object-oriented Languages

Contents

Preface

The aim of this book is to give a presentation of object-oriented languages and programming that is both general in its scope and precise in its details. The number and variety of such languages now in existence are too great for an exhaustive review to be given in a book of this size, consequently I have attempted to identify the basic concepts that are common to many languages and to illustrate these by practical examples. It is not intended as a book from which to learn how to program in an object-oriented language – specialist works are available for this – but rather to give an understanding of the principles that underlie these languages and the techniques of object-oriented programming.

Readers should have some experience of programming in one or more of the 'classical' languages such as Pascal or Lisp, or at least some familiarity with the principles of such languages. The book is addressed particularly to second- and third-year students in courses leading to a degree in computer science or in which computer science is taught as far as high-level languages. It is addressed also to students in schools of engineering, to research workers, to teachers and generally to all who would like to understand object-oriented languages.

The style and content of the presentation are based on several years' experience of teaching at the Université de Paris-Sud; the small amount of lecture time allowed for object-oriented languages made it not practical to teach a particular language in detail, and encouraged an approach in the form of a synthesis. The result was this skeletal structure, liberally illustrated with examples. The aim is to enable the reader to approach programming in an object-oriented language with a clear and accurate perception of the universe of such languages.

Many people have contributed to making the book clearer and, I hope, more readily accessible than it would have been without their help. Thomas Baudel, Jean Chassin, Stéphane Chatty, Marc Durocher and Solange Karsenty read and re-read the preliminary drafts. The members of the Human-Computer

Interaction Group in the Computer Science Research Laboratory at Paris-Sud, drawing on their daily experience of object-oriented programming, helped me to bring out more clearly the practical realities of using these languages and also tested some of the ideas I develop. Marie-Claude Gaudel helped to clarify the concepts related to typing in programming languages in general and in object-oriented languages in particular. Finally, my gratitude to my brother Emmanuel, who drew the figures, is unbounded.

Michel Beaudouin-Lafon
Université de Paris-Sud, 1991

1

Introduction

Object-oriented languages as such first appeared some years ago, as a new method of programming, but the idea of programming in terms of objects goes back to the mid-1960s, when Ole Dahl and Kristen Nygaard in Norway created the language Simula for simulating physical processes. Although much research in this field has been done since then, it is only recently that these languages have become widely accepted. The aim of this book is to show that object-oriented programming is not just a passing fashion but provides a general approach that offers many advantages.

1.1 THE FIELD OF LANGUAGES

It is not an easy task to position object-oriented languages within the broad field of programming languages since the concept conveyed by the term 'object' can vary with the context in which it is used. The languages themselves can be classified in different ways; we start by giving some of these classifications, and in each case show where object-oriented languages fit.

1.1.1 Classification of programming languages

Classification by programming model

The following are the main programming models now in general use – that is, the models used for expressing a computation.
   Imperative programming. This is the oldest style, in which the algorithm for the computation is expressed explicitly in terms of instructions such as assignments, tests, branchings and so on. Execution of the algorithm requires data values to be held in variables which the program can access and modify. The

formula due to Niklaus Wirth describes imperative languages perfectly:

program = algorithm + data structure

Languages so classified include assembly languages, Fortran, Algol, Pascal, C and Ada; the category is the oldest because it corresponds naturally to the earliest, basic model for the architecture of the computer, the von Neumann model.

Functional programming, popularized by the language Lisp, takes a much more mathematical approach, based on early work on the lambda calculus. The concept of variable is not used here, instead the computation is described as a function which is applied to the input data and which gives the result(s) as output data. This style of programming is more abstract since it requires the algorithm to be described in a way that is independent of the data. There are very few purely functional languages, because carrying this abstraction to completion gives programs that are cumbersome and very tedious to write; most languages in this class, therefore, reintroduce the concept of variable for reasons of practicality. Languages here are Lisp and its many versions, such as CommonLisp, Scheme, ... , and ML.

Logic programming, like functional programming, also takes a mathematical approach, this time through formal logic. The program is described in terms of predicates, which are the rules that govern the problem; at run time the use of logical inference enables new formulae to be derived from those given, or the truth or falsehood of a formula to be deduced from the predicates. Logical inference is very much like the process of proving a theorem in mathematics, starting from the axioms and theorems already proved. The best-known logic language is Prolog.

The question arises, should object-oriented programming be a new category in this classification? – and it is difficult to answer. Programming in terms of objects has similarities to imperative programming: in the Wirth formula, imperative programming puts the accent on the algorithmic part whilst object-oriented programming puts it on the data structure. However, this does not justify including the object-oriented languages in the imperative group, because their approach applies equally well to the functional and to the logical models.

Classification by computational method

This is an extension of the previous classification, according to two modes of execution:

Sequential languages: the instructions are executed one after another in an order that can be deduced from the text of the program. These are the most widely used languages, since they correspond to the classic von Neumann architecture which postulates a single processing unit. Most object-oriented languages are sequential.

Parallel languages: in contrast to sequential languages, several program instructions can be executed simultaneously; this has been made possible by the development of parallel-architecture machines. Parallel programming demands special languages, since the more usual sequential languages do not provide the primitives that are essential for communication and synchronization. It turns out that the general model for programming in terms of objects can be easily made parallel; and one group of object-oriented languages, that of *actor languages*, are in effect parallel languages.

Classification by typing

As the name suggests, this is based on the concept of **type**. This has been introduced into programming languages to increase security: associating a type with every expression makes it possible to establish by static analysis – that is, by a study of the program text alone and without any need to execute it – that the program is correct so far as the type system is concerned. This will ensure that the program will not fail at run time by, for example, attempting to add a boolean to an integer.

Static typing. In such a language a type is assigned to each expression as a result of a static analysis; this is the safest typing system, but the most constraining. Pascal is a typical example of such a language.

Strong typing. With such languages a static analysis of the program can show that execution will not lead to a type error, but may not be able to assign a type to every expression. Consequently some types may have to be computed at run time to control execution. Languages that offer parametric polymorphism or genericity, like Ada, are strongly typed, as are most typed object-oriented languages, notably Simula, Modula-3 and C++.

Weak typing. Here correctness with respect to the type system cannot be established by static analysis, and the types of the expressions have to be computed and checked at run time: hence the term **dynamic typing**. Eiffel is a weakly typed object-oriented language.

Untyped languages make no use of the concept of type and therefore offer no check on validity in this respect. Lisp is an untyped language, as is the object-oriented language Smalltalk.

Using a type system makes programming safer, which is essential in constructing large software systems; and further, as we shall see, it can lead to more efficient execution. It is therefore an important concept. We use it as a criterion for structuring the book, distinguishing between typed (object-oriented) languages (strongly or weakly) on the one hand and untyped languages on the other. Much work is being done at present on type systems for object-oriented languages, since the concept of inheritance, which is central here, requires systems that differ from those that have been studied so far.

Classification by mode of execution

Strictly speaking, the way in which the execution of a program is achieved is not a characteristic of the language as such but rather of the particular implementation.

Interpreted languages. With these, each expression is executed immediately after it has been entered to the machine by the user. This has the advantage of enabling the user to test and to modify the program quickly, but has the disadvantage of reducing the speed of execution. There is also the disadvantage that interpreted languages usually provide less safety than the compiled languages considered next, since many semantic checks have to be applied during the interpretation phase rather than in a preliminary compilation phase. Many object-oriented languages are interpreted and take advantage of this apparent weakness to give greater flexibility at run time. A small modification can affect the whole execution (in a controlled way) and this can be used to construct sophisticated programming environments.

Compiled languages are those for which a program has first to pass through a preliminary phase of **compilation**, the purpose of which is to produce code that is directly executable by the machine and which is therefore more efficient. If the language is typed the **compiler** that performs this can in general use information provided by the type system, and for this reason most typed languages are compiled. Writing a compiler for a language is a considerable task, especially if it is to generate efficient code, so there are many more interpreted languages than compiled; this applies to object-oriented languages as much as to others, with the consequence that not many of these are compiled.

Semi-compiled languages have the characteristics of interpreted languages but in order to improve efficiency they use a compiler behind the scenes, as it were, invisible to the user. This compiler may translate all or only parts of the program, and translates either directly into machine code or into an intermediate language that is then executed by an interpreter. Object-oriented languages that are regarded as interpreted are often in fact semi-compiled, for example Smalltalk and the prototyping language Self, both of which we describe in later chapters.

Classification by modularity

This, our last classification, concerns the way in which the language enables the programmer to modularize the program and to encapsulate the data; this is valuable because it increases safety and provides a basis for the reusability of code.

No modularity. This means that the programmer must implement modularity, using programming and naming conventions of his own. Pascal is such a language; all global variables, procedures and functions must be given different names, and definitions cannot be hidden except by means of the visibility rules (applying to nested procedures). The C language provides modularity through division of the program into separate files, by allowing variables and functions to be declared as private to a file; but it does not allow nested procedures or functions.

Explicit modularity. Some languages include the module as one of their concepts, which can be used in conjunction with other concepts of the language. In Ada, for example, the 'package' concept enables modules to be constructed and combined with 'genericity' so as to define generic modules, parametrized by types.

Implicit modularity. Object-oriented languages provide a form of modularity that can be described as implicit in that it does not make use of any particular structures of the language; in fact, the concept of module is implicit in that of class.

Programming in object-oriented languages is a form of modular programming in which the unit of modularity is strongly tied to the data structure; in contrast, Ada provides modularity in a form much less dependent on the data structures and on the processing. Modularity is often regarded as a great asset in reuse of programs, and because of this object-oriented languages are seen as allowing reuse to a much greater extent than in other languages.

1.1.2 Object-oriented programming as a style

This survey will have shown that object-orientation is more of a general approach to programming than a type that is easily classifiable. In fact, 'Object' extensions have been developed to many existing languages, for example Object Pascal, Object Lisp, Object COBOL and others. Whilst some of these extensions may not have proved very successful it remains a fact that the principles of object orientation are applicable in a wide range of contexts.

1.2 HISTORY

Figure 1.1 gives the genealogy of the main object-oriented languages; this shows that many are derived from the seminal languages Simula and Smalltalk.

1.2.1 The Simula family

As we said at the start of this chapter, Simula, the simulation language dating from the 1960s, is considered as the precursor of object-oriented languages. Simula introduced the concepts of *class* and *object*, of *method* and of *virtual method*, all of which, as we shall see in Chapter 3, are basic in typed and compiled object-

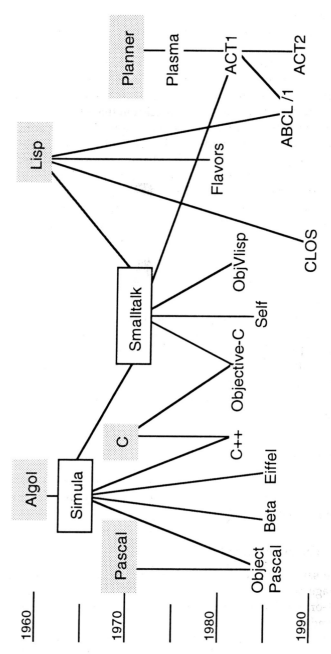

Figure 1.1 Genealogy of the main object-oriented languages.

oriented languages. It followed the line of Algol, the typed language of that period, from which Pascal also was derived.

Languages of the Simula family are imperative and typed, and generally are compiled; typing is important in that it allows many semantic checks to be applied at compile time, so reducing the number of errors detected at run time. Typing and compilation are independent concepts, so one can envisage both interpreted typed languages and compiled untyped languages, but there are few examples, since information can be deduced from the typing that enables more efficient code to be generated, and this encourages the compilation of typed languages.

Simula has inspired several object-oriented languages, some of which, for example C++ and Eiffel, have become better known and more widely used than Simula itself. Many languages have been produced by adding some or all of the concepts of object orientation to existing languages: thus Classcal and its descendent Object Pascal add classes to Pascal, Modula-3 is a major rewrite of Modula-2 with the addition of objects, and C++ is derived from C. This has both advantages and disadvantages: building on an existing language has advantages for the designers and for the users since it avoids the need for much reinventing and relearning, but the base language may prove to have features that are unfavourable to the addition of object-related mechanisms.

1.2.2   The Smalltalk family

Smalltalk, considered by many to be the prototype of object-oriented languages, was a product of research initiated by Alan Kay in the 1970s at Xerox PARC. Thus it was from Smalltalk rather than from Simula that the 1980s wave of object-oriented languages originated.

Smalltalk took the concepts of class, object and method from Simula but its approach to implementation was influenced by Lisp: it is a semi-compiled language in which everything is decided at run time. Like Lisp it exploits the flexibility provided by interpretation.

Smalltalk introduced the concept of *metaclass*, which is not present in Simula; this enables a 'metacircular' definition of the language to be given, from which it becomes fairly easy to write a Smalltalk interpreter in Smalltalk itself – a property that applies equally to Lisp and to many interpreted languages. In Smalltalk the metaclasses are accessible to the user in a natural way and provide many programming aids. This metacircularity was built into the first version, Smalltalk-72, and refined, improved and enriched in the subsequent versions Smalltalk-76 and Smalltalk-80. Other languages inspired by Smalltalk have taken the concept further, in particular ObjVLisp and Self.

The strongest evidence for the power of Smalltalk is provided by the number of programs written in the language, together with the level of research into the language itself, its concepts and the languages derived from it. Particularly noteworthy is the Smalltalk programming environment, developed at Xerox PARC and written in Smalltalk; this, which includes an operating system, was the first computer graphics environment to be taken up widely.

Smalltalk has given rise to many programming languages, many of which, unlike Smalltalk itself which is a language in its own right, are implemented in terms of Lisp, on top of which it has proved easy to add object mechanisms. It is unfortunate that in many cases the underlying language is accessible to the programmer, for this gives the possibility of programming in two largely incompatible styles, the functional style of Lisp and the object-oriented style of the Smalltalk derivative. Some versions of Lisp, for example Le_Lisp and CLOS (CommonLisp Object System) integrate object mechanisms in such a way that the result is more like a unified language.

1.2.3   Other languages and families

Whilst the Simula and Smalltalk families account for a large fraction of the object-oriented languages, there are other languages that do not fall into any particular class, and other families in course of development.

Objective-C is a **hybrid language**, combining Smalltalk-type objects with C. It is less an integration of the two than a type of coexistence of two programming universes, with the move from either to the other made explicit by means of syntactic delimiters. The entities of either universe can be transferred to the other, but they then become opaque objects that cannot be manipulated. The interest of this approach is that it offers the user two environments: a typed and compiled one, that of C, and an untyped and interpreted one, that of Smalltalk. The best-known software written in Objective-C is undoubtedly Interface Builder, an environment for developing interactive applications for the NeXT machine.

Another family is that of **prototype-based languages**. These, unlike classical object-oriented languages, are based not on the concepts of class and object but solely on that of prototype, which can have the characteristics of a class or of an object or of something intermediate between the two. In a way, such languages push the object concept to its extremes and enable new programming models to be explored.

Finally, there is the family of parallel languages called **actor languages**. Here the program is written in terms of objects called actors, each of which is a process that executes autonomously and sends and receives messages to and from other actors. After an actor has sent a message to another it can continue its execution, without any consideration of the consequence of receipt of the message; thus parallelism is introduced by means of a simple modification to the method of communication between pairs of objects. Compared with mechanisms for parallelism provided by other languages, such as the `task` mechanism of Ada, this is strikingly simple and elegant; it puts the actor languages in a special position for the exploration of parallelism.

1.3   PLAN OF THE BOOK

The prime aim of this book is to present the basic principles of object-oriented languages and the main techniques of programming in terms of objects. It does not set out to teach how to program in one or other of the existing languages, and therefore the examples are given in a pseudolanguage whose syntax is similar to that of Pascal. This makes it possible to illustrate the different concepts in a uniform manner.

Chapter 2 gives the general principles underlying object-oriented programming. The three succeeding chapters deal with the main families of languages: Chapter 3 with typed languages, the Simula family; Chapter 4 with untyped languages, in particular with Smalltalk; and Chapter 5 with prototype and actor languages. Chapter 6 ends the book with accounts of some of the techniques commonly used in object-oriented programming, and an outline of a general methodology.

A knowledge of the basic principles of programming languages in general, and of Pascal in particular, is assumed. Chapters 3 and 4 are mutually independent; the reader who prefers Lisp to Pascal could read Chapter 4 before Chapter 3.

2

Basic principles

Object-oriented languages are based on the concepts of **class** and **instance**, which may be compared to those of *type* and *variable* respectively in a language such as Pascal. A class describes the characteristics common to all its instances, in a form similar to the `record` of Pascal, and thus defines a set of **fields**. It also defines a set of **methods**, the operations that can be performed with or on its instances, and is thus an entity in itself. With an object-oriented language, instead of applying global procedures or functions to variables, we invoke the methods associated with the instances, an action often called **message passing**. In effect, we send a message to the instance requesting an operation to be performed, and the instance determines the method to be invoked.

The term 'object' is often used instead of instance. 'Instance' emphasizes membership of a class – we speak of an instance of a class – whilst 'object' refers in a general way to some entity of the program, which can be an instance but also a field, a class or some other entity.

The other basic concept is **inheritance**, the derivation of a new class from an existing class, with modifications or extensions. This is a structuring mechanism that is fundamental in object-oriented languages; it is described in section 2.3 below.

Figure 2.1 illustrates these basic concepts and gives the graphical conventions we shall use in all figures.

2.1 CLASSES AND INSTANCES

The concept of object or instance encompasses all those entities in a program written in an object-oriented language that can store a state and respond to a message. This can be compared with the concept of a variable in the traditional languages: a

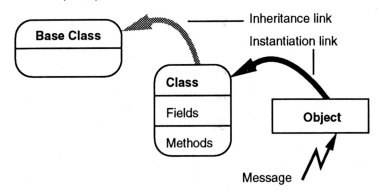

Figure 2.1 The basic concepts.

variable can store a state but cannot itself cause any processing to be performed. Processing is achieved by subprograms, functions or procedures, which take the variable(s) as parameters, may modify them, and may return values.

For example, in a traditional language the type `Stack` can be defined, together with procedures for access or modification:

`Push`   takes a stack and a value to be put on the stack.
`Pop`   takes a stack.
`Top`   takes a stack and returns a value.

This separation between variables and procedures in traditional languages is the source of many problems concerning encapsulation of data. In the interests of program safety, one does not want to have a situation in which any procedure can access the contents of any variable, and this leads to the concept of module. A module exports types, variables and procedures, and the implementations of the types are not accessible from outside the module – they are **opaque**; the variables of each type cannot be manipulated other than by means of the procedures exported by the module. The implementation of the type is defined within the module and is used there by the procedure bodies.

Thus the concept of a stack can be encapsulated in a module, which exports a type `Stack` and the procedures `Push`, `Pop` and `Top`, the implementation of which is not known outside the module. This makes it impossible for a user of the module to modify a stack except by the procedures provided, and so ensures the integrity of the stack.

A module thus provides the means for grouping types and procedures together so as to construct abstract types. This possibility is provided by Clu, Ada and ML, for example; other languages, including Pascal, Lisp and C, do not offer modularity and with these the programmer has to exercise great care in ensuring that its effects are produced by other means.

The object-oriented approach integrates the concepts of variable and of the associated procedures into that of object: this provides encapsulation immediately, without the need for any further mechanisms. Just as in a traditional language a variable belongs to a type, here an object belongs to a class. The class is simultaneously a type and a module: it contains a description of the type, in the form of fields, and a set of procedures associated with that type, called methods.

2.1.1 Definition of a class

We define a class `Stack` by:

1. a state, consisting of fields that represent the stack (array, list, etc.); thus if we use an array we shall have two fields, the array itself and the index of the current top of the stack;
2. the method `Push`, taking a value as parameter;
3. the method `Pop`;
4. the method `Top`, which returns a value.

Objects are created by a mechanism called **instantiation**. An object thus created is called an instance of the class as shown in Figure 2.2. Instantiation is similar to creating a variable of type `record`. The instance holds a state consisting of a value for each of the fields, the fields themselves being objects. All languages have a number of predefined classes, such as the class of integers, of characters, etc.

Encapsulation of objects, meaning control of access, is provided automatically by the definition of a class. Whilst the situation differs from one language to another, as we shall see, we can take it that in general the fields are private but the methods are public; this means that the fields are visible only from within the body of an object but the methods are visible

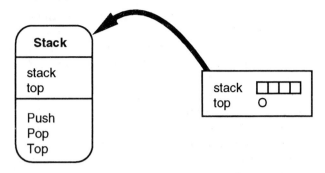

Figure 2.2 The class Stack and an instance.

from outside. We now describe the mechanism for invoking these methods.

2.2   METHODS, MESSAGE PASSING

In an object-oriented language the objects hold values and the methods provide the means for manipulating the objects. This is comparable to the situation in a traditional language, in which the variables hold the values and are manipulated by the functions and procedures, with the difference that whilst these functions and procedures are global entities of the program, the methods in an object-oriented language belong to the classes of objects. Thus instead of calling a global function or procedure, a method *belonging to an object* is invoked, and the method is executed in the context of that object.

The term message passing is often used for this process of invocation. Whilst in a traditional language we should, for example, call a procedure Push and provide as parameters the name of the stack and a value, say 20, we can view the operation here as sending the message 'Push 20' to an object, the stack in question.

This distinction is fundamental. The sending of a message implies that it is the receiver, here the stack, that decides how to implement its content, here the placing of the value 20 on the stack, by calling the corresponding method defined in its class. In contrast, in a traditional language the calling of a procedure implies that it is that procedure, here Push, that decides what is to be done with the arguments, here the stack and the value 20. In other words, imperative and functional programming privilege central control (procedures and functions) whilst object-oriented programming privileges the data (the objects) and devolves control to the objects.

The body of a method is executed in the context of the receiving object, thus giving direct access to the fields and methods of the latter without any need for further mechanisms. In fact, the private parts of an object, meaning generally its fields, although this can vary according to the language, are accessible only via the body of the methods defined in its class.

The combined definition of the fields and methods belonging to a class lies at the heart of the inheritance mechanism, which we now describe.

2.3 INHERITANCE

The concept of inheritance is a distinguishing feature of object-oriented languages: it enables new classes to be derived from those already existing.

Suppose we want to program the Towers of Hanoi game. In this there are three vertical rods (towers), on one of which are threaded a number of unequal-sized discs in decreasing order of size from the base upwards, and the game is to transfer these to one of the other rods with the following rules:

1. only one disc may be moved at a time;
2. no disc may be placed on one of smaller size.

The properties of a tower are thus similar to those of a stack, in that elements (discs) can be added or removed, one at a time; the constraint on size means that a given disc can be added only if its value (diameter) is less than that of the current stack top.

If we program this game in a traditional language that provides encapsulation we have these alternatives.

1. Represent each tower by a stack, and precede every call of the procedure Push with a check that the disc being considered for stacking satisfies the constraint on size;
2. Create a new module which exports an opaque type Tower and procedures Push, Pop, Top. Tower is implemented as a

stack, `Push` includes the check on size, and `Pop`, `Top` call the corresponding procedures defined for the stack.

Neither is satisfactory. The first provides nothing of the abstraction corresponding to the concept of the tower; the second does not have this objection but has a number of disadvantages.

1. It requires unnecessary writing of procedures: `Pop` for the module `Tower` can only call `Pop` for the module `Stack`;
2. If we add a function `Depth` to `Stack` this will not be accessible to `Tower` unless we also add to `Tower` a function `Depth`, as we have had to add `Pop`;
3. The situation is more serious if we decide to remove the function `Depth` that had been defined for `Stack`; an attempt to use this in `Tower` then calls a non-existent function;
4. The encapsulation prevents direct access to the stack in the implementation of the module `Tower`; consequently it would not be possible to add the function `Depth` to `Tower` without first defining such a function for `Stack`.

What we want is some kind of link between the modules `Stack` and `Tower` which will enable us to derive the second as a specialization of the first. This is achieved by the inheritance mechanism, which enables us to define a class `Tower` by inheriting from `Stack` as illustrated in Figure 2.3.

2.3.1   Defining a class by inheritance

If a class `B` inherits from a class `A`, then the instances of `B` contain the same fields as do those of `A` and the methods of `A` are available in `B`. In addition, the subclass `B` may:

1. define new fields to add to those inherited from the base class `A`;
2. define new methods, similarly added to those inherited from `A`;
3. redefine (i.e. modify) any of the methods inherited from `A`.

Further, any methods defined or redefined in `B` have access to the fields and methods of both `B` and `A`.

These are the properties of the special relation that links `B` to `A`. One consequence is that there is no need to modify `B` to take

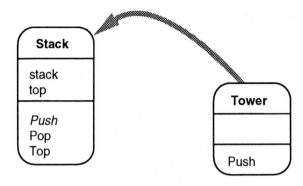

Figure 2.3 The class `Tower` inherited from the class `Stack`.

account of any fields and/or methods that may be added to A, and correspondingly for deletions from A – provided, of course, that none of the methods of B uses any of the deleted material.

In the previous example we have only redefined the method `Push` to include a check of the size of the disc before calling `Push` from `Stack`, so as to ensure that the operation is valid (Figure 2.3). We say therefore that we have **specialized** the class `Stack`, for all we have done is to redefine one of its methods. If in addition we had defined any new methods for `Tower` – for example, had included initialization with a set of discs ordered in decreasing size – then we should have **enriched** the class `Stack`. This simple example shows that inheritance can be used to achieve two effects, specialization and enrichment.

2.3.2 The inheritance tree

As we have presented it, inheritance generates a forest of trees of classes. Each class is a node in the forest; its parent is its base class and its children are its subclasses. The roots of the trees are the classes that do not inherit from any other class.

If C inherits from B and B inherits from A we say that C inherits **indirectly** from A. We can express the inheritance relation between A and B in any of the following ways:

1. B inherits from A
2. B is a subclass of A

3.   B derives/is derived from A
4.   B is a derived class of A
5.   A is a (the) superclass of B
6.   A is a (the) base class of B.

In the two last definitions the definite article is used when A is the direct antecedent of B in the inheritance tree.

Some languages postulate a single base class from which all other classes are derived, often calling this simply Object. The inheritance relation then defines not a forest but a single tree; in all cases, however, we use the term loosely and speak of the inheritance tree.

2.4   MULTIPLE INHERITANCE

The inheritance just defined is called simple inheritance, meaning that any class has at most one base class; this generalizes to multiple inheritance, in which a class can inherit directly from several classes, with the following properties:

If class B inherits from classes A1, A2, ..., An, then

1.   the fields of the instances of B are the union of B's own fields and the fields of A1, A2, ..., An;
2.   the methods defined for the instances of B are the union of the methods defined in B and those defined in A1, A2, ..., An. B can of course redefine any of the methods of its base classes.

The inheritance tree or forest now becomes a graph; to avoid circular definitions this graph is not allowed to have cycles, that is, no class may be a subclass of itself, directly or indirectly,

The generalization to multiple inheritance seems simple but in fact can lead to many difficulties, in particular concerning conflicts of names of inherited fields and methods. We shall have to leave the discussion of some of these difficulties to the more detailed treatments of the later chapters.

One difficulty inherent in multiple inheritance is the management of repeated inheritance of a particular class. If B and C inherit (simply) from A, and D inherits from B and from C, then D inherits from A by each of two routes, D–B–A and D–C–A (Figure 2.4): should an instance of D have two sets of the fields

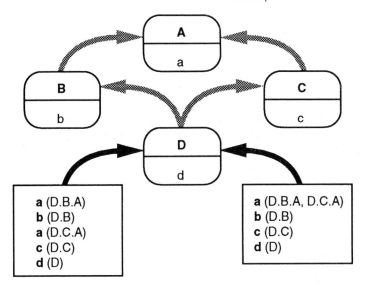

Figure 2.4 Two interpretations of multiple inheritence.

defined in A, or should a single set share the responsibilities of the two routes? The following simple examples show that the choice can depend on the situation being studied.

1. Suppose A is the class of sources of motive power (motors), whose fields give the characteristics of the motors; and that B and C are the classes of automobiles and of cranes respectively. Then D is the class of mobile cranes and there are two possibilities. If D inherits the class of motors twice, once by each route, then the mobile crane has two motors, one to move the vehicle and one to operate the crane; if only once, it has a single motor to perform both tasks. Either choice could be valid, and which is appropriate depends on the circumstances.

2. Suppose A is the class of moveable objects, whose fields include position and speed; B the class of ships, with various fields (tonnage for example); and C the class of wind-driven objects, one of whose fields is the area of the sail. Then D is the class of sailing ships, and any instance of D can at any

time have only one position and only one speed; therefore only one set of these fields should be inherited from A.

Multiple inheritance does not provide a satisfactory solution to such problems. The first interpretation (inheriting twice) corresponds to a **composition** of classes, the second to a **combination**. The inheritance mechanism is certainly not perfect for capturing simultaneously the concepts of specialization, enrichment, composition and combination. However, inheritance is not the only means for defining classes. One of the traps into which the user of an object-oriented language can fall is the wrong use of inheritance. The question that should be asked whenever a class is defined is this: should B inherit from A, or should B contain a field that is an instance of A? – is B a kind of A, or does it contain an A? We shall return to this problem in Chapter 6 where we consider the practice of object-oriented programming.

2.5 POLYMORPHISM

The concept of polymorphism concerns the capability a language has for describing the behaviour of a procedure in a way that does not depend on the nature of its parameters. Thus a procedure that exchanges the values of two variables is polymorphic if it can be written so as to be independent of the types of the variables; so is the procedure Push if it does not depend on the type of the value that is to be put on the stack.

Since it is defined with respect to types, polymorphism is relevant only to typed languages. There are three kinds as follows:

1. *Ad hoc* polymorphism is achieved by writing the procedure body afresh for each of the types that will be encountered – this is often called **overloading**. Thus separate, independent, procedures could be defined for Swap (Integer, Integer) and for Swap (Disc, Disc), or for Push (Stack, Integer) and Push (Stack, Disc). The selection of the version(s) to be used on any particular occasion is generally made statically, that is, at compile time, by noting the types of the parameters in the procedure call.

2. Inclusive polymorphism is based on a partial ordering of the types: if type B comes below type A in this relation then an

object of type B will be accepted by a procedure written to expect a type A. A single procedure is then equivalent to a whole family, one for every type below that for which it is written. Thus if Integer and Disc are below Object in the ordering we need only to write, for example, the procedure Swap (Object, Object) or Push (Stack, Object) in order to handle all three types.

3. Parametric polymorphism employs genericity, in which types are used as parameters: a model of the procedure is defined and is implemented on any particular occasion with the types relevant to that occasion. Thus if a procedure Swap (<T>, <T>) is written it can be implemented with <T> = Integer or <T> = Disc as needed; and similarly for Push (Stack, <T>)

All three types of polymorphism occur in one or other of the traditional languages. Polymorphism exists in Pascal but is not accessible to the user; being implicit it cannot be classified according to the above definitions. For example, the arithmetical operators are polymorphic since they can be applied equally to integers, to reals and even to sets; so are the input/output procedures read and write, which will accept parameters of different types.

Ada offers *ad hoc* polymorphism through the possibility of overloading the names of procedures and operators, and parametric polymorphism through the provision for defining generic functions. The scope for inclusive polymorphism, however, is limited; for only very few types can an ordering relation be defined.

2.5.1 Polymorphism in object-oriented languages

The definition of polymorphism involves the concept of type, but not all object-oriented languages are typed. A typed object-oriented language is one in which each class defines a type and in which the type of every object used is declared explicitly; the possibility of both *ad hoc* and inclusive polymorphism in these languages follows naturally. Some typed languages offer parametric polymorphism also, but we shall not consider this in this chapter.

Ad hoc polymorphism allows two methods in two independent classes – that is, classes not linked by inheritance – to have the same name. The bodies of the two methods are defined independently in the respective classes and the user can send the same message to each of two objects, one in each of the two classes. This type of polymorphism is intrinsic to object-oriented languages; no special mechanism is required, and the possibility follows immediately from the fact that every object is responsible for the handling of any message that it receives.

A different form of *ad hoc* polymorphism is the use of the same name for different methods in the same class or in classes related by inheritance; this is not offered implicitly by all object-oriented languages, although many do offer it through the possibility of overloading. Redefinition of a method in a derived class, with the same name and the same parameters as in the base class, does not constitute overloading but a redefinition, as we saw in the description of inheritance (Section 2.3.1)

Inclusive polymorphism (often called inheritance polymorphism) is provided naturally by object-oriented languages. Simple inheritance generates a hierarchy of classes and thus a partial ordering: if B inherits from A, directly or indirectly, then we can say that B is below A in the order relation and any method of A can be applied to an object of class B. This allows us to apply the method Top of the class Stack to an object of class Tower, since Tower is a subclass of Stack.

Inheritance polymorphism can be defined for multiple inheritance also, by constructing a partial ordering of the classes that is compatible with the inheritance graph. This graph has no cycles; therefore if for any pair of classes A and B a directed path can be found joining B to A we can say that B is below A; there is no risk of inconsistency, because the absence of cycles means that if there is a directed path from B to A there cannot be one from A to B. Thus the essential antisymmetry property is ensured.

This polymorphism applies not only to the receivers of messages but equally to the passing of the parameters of the messages: a message that takes a formal parameter of class A will accept an actual parameter of class B provided that B is below A in the hierarchy. Thus if the method Push is written for a parameter of class Integer it can be given a parameter of class Disc if Disc inherits from Integer.

2.5.2 Static and dynamic binding

Inheritance polymorphism removes the possibility of static typing from object-oriented languages: an object declared in class A can, at run time, contain an object of a subclass of A. Thus these languages are at best strongly typed, and this has important consequences for compilation. If the typing is static the compiler can decide the method to be called in response to a message, giving what is called static binding; if it is not then the decision must be made at run time and we have dynamic binding, losing an important advantage of static typing, the efficiency of the code generated.

Dynamic binding must be used with untyped languages, since then the absence of typing prevents any a priori determination of the method to be called. Techniques have been developed for both cases to improve the efficiency, which we shall consider later.

The close ties between polymorphism, typing and mode of linking determine to a large extent the compromises made in different languages between power of expression, safety of programming and efficiency at run time. No existing language is ideal in the sense that it gives the best compromise in every case, and it is unlikely that such an ideal language can exist.

2.6 METACLASSES

So far our definition of an object has been rather vague, as all that we have said is that an object must belong to a class. Some languages allow a class to be regarded as an object, in which case that class itself must be an instance of some class: the class of a class is then called a **metaclass** (Figure 2.5).

The description of a class that we have given is similar to that of an object: a class contains the list of the names of the fields of its instances and a dictionary of methods that can be applied to these instances. The fields of a metaclass are (a) the names of the fields of the class and (b) the dictionary of methods. Since instantiation is a method that can be performed by a class, this will be one of the methods of the metaclass.

In addition, a metaclass can hold other fields and methods. For example, the inheritance tree is a relation between classes and

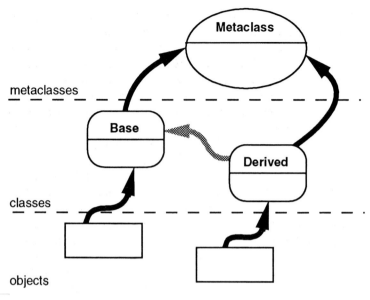

Figure 2.5 The metaclass concept.

each class contains a field which designates its base class – this is shown by the grey arrows in the diagrams; one method defined for a class is a test to determine if it is a subclass of another class.

Several models have been proposed for metaclasses. In the simplest there is only one, called, for example, Metaclass, whilst at the other extreme metaclasses can be defined arbitrarily; this allows, for example, instantiation to be redefined or class methods to be defined in the metaclass. An intermediate model, that of Smalltalk-80, envisages a single metaclass for each class, with the programming environment responsible for creating the metaclass for each class created by the programmer; this enables class methods to be defined and stored in the metaclass's dictionary. This last approach makes metaclasses effectively transparent to the programmer and provides a satisfactory compromise in most applications.

The metaclass concept, however, could generate an infinite regress: a metaclass is a class and therefore an object, and therefore belongs to a class, which is an object, ... The regression is short-circuited by introducing a cycle in the instantiation tree, for example by making Metaclass its own metaclass. Metaclasses have two very different applications. The first is to allow a metacircular definition of a language and so make its execution structures accessible: this is called **reification**. Lisp has this property, making it easy to write a Lisp interpreter in Lisp. In a reified language it is easy also to construct means for self-inspection which will help in implementing programs: tracing the routes of messages, calls of methods, changes of values of variables, etc.

The second is to enable classes to be constructed dynamically. Consider for example an interactive graphics system in which the user can construct new graphics objects that can be used in a similar way to the primitive objects: for example, circles, rectangles, etc. Each new object, when turned into a model, leads to the creation of a new class and each such creation can be performed as an instantiation of an existing metaclass. Without the metaclass the mechanism would have to be simulated in some way or another, which could be tedious.

The availability of metaclasses in an object-oriented language means that new classes can be defined dynamically (i.e. at run time) and existing classes modified. This prohibits static typing and explains why metaclasses are available only in untyped languages. Some typed languages, however, use the concept implicitly, for example by allowing the methods of instantiation to be redefined; and objects can be defined which act as meta-classes for representing the inheritance tree at run time. But only untyped languages can exploit the full power of metaclasses.

3

Typed object-oriented languages

We now take up the subject of typed object-oriented languages. Simula is the ancestor of these but is little used today, so we shall base our discussion on the more recent languages C++, Eiffel and Modula-3. The first version of C++ was defined in 1983 by Bjarne Stroustrup at Bell Labs, where both C and UNIX originated; Eiffel was begun in 1985 by Bertrand Meyer of Software Engineering Inc.; and the development of Modula-3, a new version of Modula, was begun by Luca Cardelli and Greg Nelson at the DEC Systems Research Centre in 1988.

For our examples we shall use a pseudolanguage with a syntax, based largely on that of Pascal, which we hope will appear natural. The following is a description of this language in extended BNF, in which the following conventions are used.

1. Keywords are in bold type.
2. Other terminals are in italics.
3. Square brackets denote optional parts.
4. Vertical bars separate alternatives.
5. Parentheses group parts of rules.
6. Indexing with + denotes repetition at least once.
7. Indexing with * denotes possible repetition, including none.
8. When the number of repetitions thus indicated exceeds 1 the index is followed by either a comma or a semicolon according to which is to be used to separate consecutive elements.

Formal description of the language

```
prog      :: = (class | method)⁺
class     :: = id-cls = class [id-cls*ʼ] {
                   [fields field⁺]
                   [methods methods⁺]
              }
field     :: = id-field⁺ʼ : type;
methods   :: = procedure id-proc (param*ʼ);
             | function id-func (param*ʼ) : type;
type      :: = id-cls | integer | boolean
             | array [const . . const] of type
param     :: = id-param⁺ʼ : type;
method    :: = procedure   id-cls.id-proc   (param*ʼ)
               block
             | function id-cls.id-func (param*ʼ):
               type block
block     :: = {[decl⁺] instr*ʼ}
decl      :: = id-var⁺ʼ : type;
instr     :: = var := expr
             | [var.]id-proc (expr*ʼ)
             | while expr-bool do instr
             | if expr-bool then body[else instr]
             | for id-var := expr to expr do instr
             | return [expr]
             | block
var       :: = id(.id-field)* | var [expr]
id        :: = id-var | id-param | id-field
expr      :: = var | const
             | [var.]id-func(expr*ʼ)
             | expr (+|-|*|/) expr
expr-bool :: = expr (<|>|=|≠) expr
             | expr-bool (and | or) expr-bool
             | not expr-bool
```

Finally, there is the convention that a line beginning with two dashes (--) is a comment (i.e. is not for execution), and that the comment continues to the end of the line.

3.1 CLASSES, OBJECTS, METHODS

3.1.1 Definition of a class

The concept of an object `class` is a natural extension of the concept of the type `record`: a class contains the description of a list of fields, supplemented by the description of a set of methods. Thus the class `Stack` that we have been discussing can be expressed:

```
Stack = class {
  fields
      stack: array[1 .. N] of integer;
      top:   integer;
  methods
      procedure Push (value: integer);
      procedure Pop ( );
      function  Top ( ): integer;
}
```

Declaration of an object corresponds to an instantiation:

```
p1: Stack;
```

The 'point' operator, << . >>, used in classical languages to access the fields of a record, is used here to invoke the methods associated with an object. Thus we can regard the methods as being manipulated as fields of the object:

```
p1.Push (10);
p1.Push (15);
p1.Pop ( );
s := p1.Top ( );   -- value of s = 10
```

This notation shows clearly the receiver of the message (here p1), the method invoked (here e.g. `Push`) and its parameter(s) (here e.g. `10`). Since there must always be a receiver for any message sent, methods can only be invoked through the means of this point notation; and, for example, the message

```
Push (10);
```

makes no sense, since no receiver is given. However, there are circumstances in which the receiver can be taken as implied, as we shall see later.

The point notation is used also to access the fields of an object:

```
p1.stack [5];
```

but in general such access will be denied by the visibility rules. As we saw in Chapter 2, whilst the methods of an object are public its fields are private, that is, whilst the methods can be accessed by any other object simply by the sending of a message, the fields can be accessed only by the object itself.

3.1.2   Definition of the methods

The names of the methods associated with a class are listed in the declaration of that class; the bodies of these methods are given separately. We use the notation class.method to specify the method completely; this allows the same name to be used for methods in different classes – an example of the *ad hoc* polymorphism defined in Chapter 2.

The declaration of method bodies is expressed differently in different languages. We shall use a notation based on that of C++. Eiffel uses a different convention, putting the declarations in a block associated with the class in which they are defined; this can be expressed in our pseudolanguage as follows:

```
Stack = class {
  procedure Push (value: integer) {
    -- body of Push
  }
    -- etc.
}
```

The two-part notation we have adopted enables the declaration of the class to be separated from that of the body of the method; however, the two notations are strictly equivalent.

Using this notation for the previous example, and omitting all tests for validity of the operations (stack full/empty), we have the following definitions for the method bodies:

```
procedure Stack.Push (value: integer) {
  -- NB: no test for overflow
  top : = top + 1;
  stack[top] := value;
}
procedure Stack.Pop ( ) {
  -- NB: no test for stack empty
  top := top - 1;
}
function Stack.Top ( ): integer {
  return stack[top];
}
```

A receiver object is always named when a method is invoked, and acts as the context for the execution. Access to the fields of this object − stack and top in the example − is gained by simply giving their names; in fact, the following are accessible from within a method:

1. the receiver object;
2. the fields of the receiver object;
3. the methods of the receiver object;
4. the parameters of the method;
5. the local variables of the method;
6. the globally declared objects of the program.

The fields and parameters are themselves objects whose methods can be invoked in turn. To illustrate this, let us assume there is a class File with a method Write and define further methods for the class Stack, to be added to those already declared:

```
procedure Stack.Write (output: File) {
  for i := 1 to top do output.Write (stack[i]);
}
procedure Stack.Clear ( ) {
  while top > 0 do Pop ( );
}
```

Stack.Write invokes the method Write with the parameter output and writes the elements of the stack to the file. Stack.Clear invokes the method Pop without stating a receiver: this seems contrary to the general principle that a

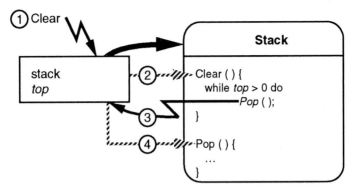

Figure 3.1 Access to fields and methods. Hachured arrows represent invocation of the method.

receiver must always be declared, but here we are working in the context of a receiver object of the class Stack, and this can be taken as the implied receiver for Pop as shown in Figure 3.1. Similarly top here is to be taken as meaning the field top of the object receiving the message.

3.1.3   The pseudovariable me

Whilst the receiver object for a method may be implicit so far as access to its fields and methods is concerned, it may in some circumstances have to be referred to explicitly, for example in order to pass it as a parameter to another method. Different languages use different names for such a reference: self in Modula-3 and Smalltalk, Current in Eiffel, this in C++; we shall use me. The name does not, strictly speaking, denote an object, but is rather a way of referring to the receiver of the method then being executed; we may call it a pseudovariable.

The following example illustrates the use of me. The classes Vertex and Arc enable a graph to be represented: a vertex is linked to a set of arcs and an arc joins a pair of vertices.

```
Vertex = class {
  fields
    -- representation of adjacent arcs
  methods
    procedure Add (a: Arc);
}
```

```
Arc = class {
  fields
    start, finish: Vertex;
  methods
    procedure Join (s1, s2: Vertex)
}
```

The body of the method `Join` of the class `Arc` is as follows:

```
procedure Arc.Join (s1, s2: Vertex) {
  start := s1;
  finish := s2;
  s1.Add (me);
  s2.Add (me);
}
```

This example shows that it is essential to be able to refer explicitly to the receiver of a message in the body of that message when it is invoked: here the arc which receives the message `Join` has to be added to the vertices `s1, s2`.

The pseudovariable `me` could be used to qualify the fields of the local methods, but that would do nothing more than encumber the notation: thus the method `Clear` of the class `Stack` could be written

```
procedure Stack.Clear ( ) {
  while me.top > 0 do me.Pop ( );
}
```

3.1.4 Primitive classes

In defining the class `Stack` we have used fields of type `integer` and type `array` respectively, regarding these types as predefined in the language. The status of predefined types varies from one language to another; in general, atomic types (`integer`, `boolean`, `character`) are not classes and cannot be inherited, whilst structured types such as `array` can sometimes be treated as generic classes.

It is always possible to construct a class that contains a field of predefined type, but unfortunately, unless there is some implicit mechanism for conversion between atomic types and classes, such a class cannot be used transparently. For example, suppose we define a class `Integer` containing a field of type `integer` as follows:

```
Integer = class {
  fields
    value: integer;
  methods
    procedure Value (v: integer);
}
procedure Integer.Value (v: integer) {
  value := v;
}
```

and that in the class `Stack` we change the type `integer` into the class `Integer`; then we can no longer write

```
p1.Push (10);
```

since `10` is not an object of the class `Integer` but a value of the predefined type `integer`. Unless some special conversion mechanism has been provided we must write

```
v: Integer;
v.Value (10);
p1.Push (v);
```

The difference in status between classes and atomic types is a consequence of compromises made in the implementation of a typed object-oriented language in the interest of efficiency; this is intellectually unsatisfying, but presents few problems in practice.

3.2   INHERITANCE

We now turn to the implementation of one of the basic concepts of object-oriented languages, inheritance; we consider its two main uses, specialization and enrichment.

3.2.1   Specialization by inheritance

We now define a subclass `Tower` of the class `Stack`: a tower is a stack of decreasing values.

```
Tower = class Stack {
  methods
    procedure Initialize (n: integer);
    function CanPush (value: integer): boolean;
    procedure Push (value: integer);
}
```

Comparing this declaration with that of the class `Stack` we see that the inheritance is stated in the heading.

The procedure `Initialize` places n discs on the tower in order of decreasing size:

```
procedure Tower.Initialize (n: integer) {
  top := 0;
  for i := n to 1 do Push (i);
}
```

`Initialize` invokes the method `Push`, which is redefined for `Tower`, using the function `CanPush`:

```
function Tower.CanPush (value: integer): boolean {
  if top = 0
    then return true;
    else return value < Top ( );
}
```

The method `CanPush` references the field `top` of its base class and also the method `Top` defined in that class. It tests the legality of the proposed addition to the tower, that is, if the tower is empty (in which case any addition is legal) or if not, if the proposed value is less than the current tower top. `Push` uses `CanPush` to decide the issue:

```
procedure Tower.Push (value: integer) {
  if CanPush (value)
    then Stack.Push (value);
    else error.Write ("push impossible");
}
```

Here we have assumed the existence of a global object `error` of the class `File`, containing a method `Write` by means of which messages can be sent to the user.

The call of `Stack.Push (value)` needs some explanation. The class `Tower` is a specialization of the class `Stack` in that it has been derived from the latter by redefining one method. In such a situation the redefined method will often need to reference the (original) method of the same name in the base class; if we wrote

```
Push (value)
```

we should initiate a recursive call, since we are in the body of the method `Push` of the class `Tower`. The notation

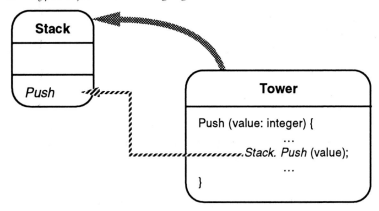

Figure 3.2 Specialization of the method Push.

```
Stack.Push (value)
```

enables us to qualify the name of the method called; since Tower
inherits from Stack, the method Push of Stack is accessible in
the current context but is hidden by the redefinition in the class
Tower as shown in Figure 3.2. The qualifying notation allows
access to the method in the base class in the context of the
receiver object; it can be used only in this situation.

Once the class Tower has been defined, instances can be
declared and its methods invoked, e.g.:

```
t: Tower;
    ...
t.Push (10)
t.Pop;
t.Push (20);
t.Push (25);   -- push impossible
```

As we have said, the methods of the base class are accessible
from the instances: here, t.Pop invokes Stack.Pop.

3.2.2   Enrichment by inheritance

We now define a derived class of Tower by adding the
possibility of graphical representation. For this we assume the
existence of classes Window and Rectangle with the following
skeleton definitions:

```
Window = class {
  methods
    procedure Clear ( );
}

Rectangle = class {
  methods
    procedure Centre (posX, posY: integer);
    procedure Size (length, height: integer);
    procedure Draw (w: Window);
}
```

TowerG is a subclass of Tower defined as follows:

```
TowerG = class Tower {
  fields
    w: Window;
    x,y: integer;
  methods
    procedure Place (posX, posY: integer);
    procedure Draw ( );
    procedure Push (value: integer);
    procedure Pop ( );
}
```

TowerG is an *enrichment* of Tower. Three new fields specify the window on the screen in which the tower is to be drawn and the position of the tower in this window. Each disc is depicted as a rectangle whose width is proportional to the integer value that represents it in the tower. Two new methods enable a position to be given and the tower to be drawn; and the methods Push and Pop have been redefined so as to ensure that the tower is redrawn at each stage of its construction. The bodies of these new methods are as follows.

Place assigns the position of the tower, and redraws it:

```
procedure TowerG.Place (posX, posY: integer) {
  x := posX;
  y := posY;
  Draw ( );
}
```

Draw starts by clearing the window and then redraws the tower, level by level; it is similar in principle to Write, defined above for the class Stack.

```
procedure TowerG.Draw ( ) {
  rect: Rectangle;
  w.Clear ( );
  for i := 1 to top do {
      rect.Centre (x, y - i);
      rect.Size (stack[i], 1);
      rect.Draw (w);
  }
}
```

Push, Pop invoke the methods of the same name in the base class Tower and redraw the tower.

```
procedure TowerG.Push (value: integer) {
  Tower.Push (value);
  Draw ( );
}
procedure TowerG.Pop ( ) {
  Tower.Pop( );
  Draw ( );
}
```

Note that Tower.Pop has not been defined: Tower inherits from Stack, so Tower.Pop is identical to Stack.Pop. However, it would be inadvisable to use Stack.Pop directly since Pop might need to be redefined in Tower.

3.3   MULTIPLE INHERITANCE

The mechanism of multiple inheritance enables a class to inherit from a number of base classes. Our class TowerG provides an example. We defined this as a tower that can draw a representation of itself in a window on the screen, but if we change our point of view slightly we can consider it as both a tower and a window, and this corresponds to multiple inheritance from Tower and Window as shown in Figure 3.3:

We now define the class TowerGM as follows.

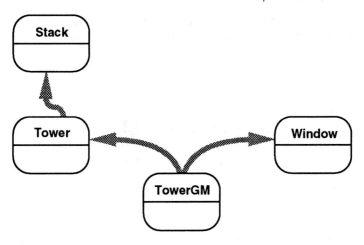

Figure 3.3 Multiple inheritance for TowerGM.

```
TowerGM = class Tower, Window {
  fields
    x,y: integer;
  methods
    procedure Place (posX, posY: integer);
    procedure Draw ( );
    procedure Push (value: integer);
    procedure Pop ( );
}
```

The multiple inheritance is declared by giving the names of the base classes in the heading of the declaration; the field w no longer appears, having been replaced by inheritance from the class Window.

The only change of method from TowerG is in Draw:

```
procedure TowerGM.Draw ( ) {
  rect: Rectangle;
  Clear ( );
  for i := 1 to top do {
      rect.Centre (x, y - 1);
      rect.Size (stack[i], 1);
      rect.Draw (me);
  }
}
```

Notice that the call of Clear is not qualified by the field w, for now this method is inherited from the class Window; whilst Draw is called with the pseudovariable me as argument. Since the class TowerGM inherits from Window, any instance is a window. Rect.Draw(me) uses inheritance polymorphism over its argument, which is expected to be of class Window.

Although the implementations of TowerG and TowerGM differ only slightly, the effect of the multiple inheritance is greater than one might think. Whilst TowerG inherits the methods of Tower only, TowerGM inherits those of both Tower and Window, so we can write

```
tgm: TowerGM;
  . . .
tgm.Place (100, 100)
tgm.Push (20);
tgm.Push (10);
tgm.Clear ( );
```

Here the call of Clear is correct, since this method is inherited from Window, whereas it would have been illegal for an object of the class TowerG. It follows that the choice between TowerG and TowerGM for implementation of a graphical tower depends on the context in which this is to be used in the particular application. A general principle is that inheritance, like multiple inheritance, should not be used as a means for simplifying implementation but as a way of specifying particular links between classes.

However, multiple inheritance can lead to ambiguities. Suppose the class Window has a method Write that prints its state. Tower inherits from Stack a method also called Write, so TowerGM inherits Write from both Tower and Window. What happens if we write

```
tgm.Write (file); ...?
```

Such conflicts are resolved differently in different languages as follows.

1. A priority relation between classes may be determined by the order in which the inheritances occur; here TowerGM inherits first from Tower and then from Window, so

`Tower.Write` hides `Window.Write` and the result is to print the state of the tower, that is, of the stack.

2. In Modula-3 and C++ the invocation of the method must be qualified, for example as `tgm.Window.Write` `(file);` this requires the user to know the inheritance graph, which runs counter to the concepts of encapsulation and abstraction.

3. The solution in Eiffel, available also in C++, is to rename the methods which will lead to these conflicts, at the time of the inheritance; thus `Write` inherited from `Window` could be renamed `WriteW`, when `tgm.Write` `(file)` would print the tower and `tgm.WriteW` `(file)` would print the window.

4. A new method `Write` could be defined in the class `TowerGM`; this would hide both the existing methods and so remove any conflict.

This last solution is always available; in our example we could define the new method as follows:

```
procedure TowerGM.Write (output: File) {
    Tower.Write (output);
    Window.Write (output);
    output.Write (x);
    output.Write (y);
}
```

This writes the parts `Tower` and `Window` and the fields belonging to `TowerGM`, thus resolving any ambiguity, and at the same time prevents the recursive call of `TowerGM.Write`.

The same conflicts arise when the same field name is used in several different base classes; they are resolved in C++ by qualification and in Eiffel by renaming.

In the preceding chapter we mentioned other problems that can arise in multiple inheritance, and in particular in repeated inheritance: what happens if a class inherits several times from the same class, directly or indirectly? Should the fields of this class be replicated or should they appear only once?

C++ provides the concept of virtual base class; this enables a base class accessible by several inheritance routes to be inherited only once. Eiffel provides finer control: if a base class is inherited several times each of its fields can be either replicated or shared according to whether it is renamed or not.

3.4   DYNAMIC BINDING

As we have presented it, inheritance of methods in a typed object-oriented language enables the invocation of the methods to be determined statically, that is, at compile time. Thus for an object o of a class A the call

```
o.m (parameters)
```

is implemented by searching A for a method of name m; if this is not found then a search is made of the base class of A, and so on, until either the method is found or the root of the inheritance tree is reached. If the search succeeds the invocation is correct, if not there is an error.

The search gives a check on the correctness of the program. The compiler can take advantage of it by generating the code that calls the method if it is found, thus avoiding the need for a similar search at run time and so improving the efficiency of the program. This is called static binding.

Unfortunately, this possibility of optimization is invalidated by inheritance polymorphism, as the following example shows.

```
t:  Tower;
tg: TowerG;
   . . .
t:= tg;
t.Push (10);   -- what happens?
```

The assignment of the graphical tower tg to the simple tower t is correct by inheritance polymorphism: a graphical tower is a particular case of a tower and therefore an object of type tower can reference a graphical tower. With static binding the compiler implements the call of Push by calling Tower.Push, since t is declared to be of type Tower. But at execution time t contains an object of class TowerG, so what should be called is TowerG.Push, and the implementation is invalid.

The example shows that static binding can prevent us from finding that an object declared to be of one class may at run time contain an object of a subclass, and so can contravene the semantics of inheritance polymorphism.

3.4.1 Virtual methods

The possibility that this problem could arise was realized during the development of Simula, and is dealt with in that language by introducing the concept of a virtual method. In our example, by declaring `Push` virtual we indicate that the binding is to be dynamic, not static: type checking is to be done as usual at compile time but the method to be called is to be determined at run time, taking account of the actual type of the object. Clearly, dynamic binding is more expensive than static binding, but its use is essential if the semantics of inheritance polymorphism is to be preserved.

The following example gives another situation in which the use of virtual methods is essential:

```
tg: TowerG;
tg.Initialize (4);
```

This initializes a graphical tower with 4 discs, and we show that here again `Push` must be declared virtual.

The procedure `Initialize` is inherited from `Tower` and has been defined as follows:

```
procedure Tower.Initialize: (n: integer) {
    for i := n to 1 do Push (i);
}
```

If `Push` has not been declared virtual it will be invoked by static binding, by means of a call to `Tower.Push`, since the receiver of the message will be considered to be of the class `Tower`. But when `tg.Initialize (4)` is invoked the receiver is in fact of the class `TowerG`, so the wrong version of `Push` will have been called, as shown in Figure 3.4. The error is avoided by declaring `Push` to be virtual, for then the version `TowerG.Push` will be called and the tower will be drawn as the initialization proceeds.

The widespread use of polymorphism in object-oriented languages could suggest that all methods should be declared virtual, and in fact this is the policy adopted in Eiffel and Modula-3, in which languages the programmer can be certain that everything happens as though the binding were always dynamic.

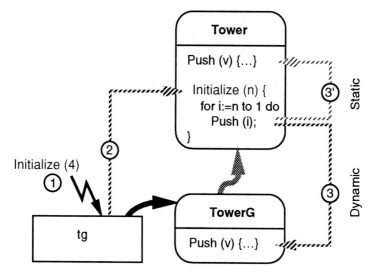

Figure 3.4 Static versus dynamic binding.

In C++ and Simula, however, virtual methods must always be declared explicitly as such, so the programmer can always choose between the security of dynamic binding and the greater efficiency of static binding with all its risks and perils. In practice few methods need to be declared virtual, but it is difficult to decide which, particularly when the classes will have to be reused.

3.4.2   Implementing dynamic binding

In the usual implementation of dynamic binding each virtual method is given an index which identifies it uniquely in the hierarchy of classes to which it belongs. At run time each class is represented by a table which gives for each index the address of the corresponding method for that class. Each object belonging to a class that contains virtual methods contains the address of this table as shown in Figure 3.5. Invoking a method is then a simple matter of indirect addressing in the table.

The cost of the implementation is thus made up as follows:

1. one table (the virtual table) for each class;
2. a pointer to this table for each object;
3. the indirect addressing for a virtual method.

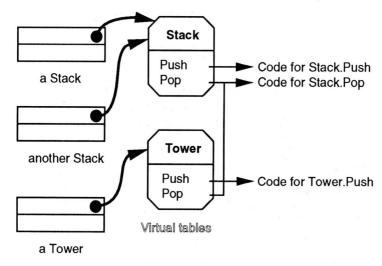

Figure 3.5 Implementation of dynamic binding.

We may consider this an acceptable cost, especially in comparison with the cost of invoking methods in untyped languages (as discussed in Chapter 4, end of section 4.3); but equally we feel that it should not be incurred for every invocation, and this is why C++ and Simula leave to the programmer the decision of which methods to declare virtual, and therefore the responsibility for the consequences of that decision. Modula-3, on the other hand, takes advantage of the virtual table needed by every object to enable an object to redefine its methods; it is sufficient to create a virtual table for each such object. This is departing from the class based languages since now the class no longer determines the behaviour of all its instances.

3.5   VISIBILITY RULES

The explicit declaration of types in a language enables errors to be detected at compile time and so gives the programmer some protection against his own mistakes. Further protection is provided by the visibility rules, that is, the encapsulation mechanisms which limit the access to fields and methods. The main purpose of encapsulation is to hide the details of the implementation of a class and so prevent an external user from changing these; it also allows changes to be made to the hidden parts without affecting the users. So far we have taken the visibility rules to be the following.

1. The fields of a class are visible only to the bodies of the methods of that class and its derived classes.
2. The methods of a class are visible to any user of the class.

3.5.1   Unit of encapsulation: class or object

Rule 1 above is ambiguous: if m is a method of a class A it can be interpreted in either of two ways.

1a. Within the body of m access can be made to the fields of any object whatever of class A, in particular to those of the receiver of m.
1b. Within the body of m access can be made only to the fields of its receiver. Thus if m has a parameter that is an object of class A, m cannot access the fields of this parameter.

These correspond to two different **visibility domains**. For 1b, the more restrictive, this domain is the object: an object is known only to the methods of its class and a method knows only the fields of its receiver. For 1a it is the whole class: a class knows all its instances and therefore every method of the class knows every instance of that class. Languages of the Simula family use 1a and thus take the unit of encapsulation to be the class, whilst those of the Smalltalk family use 1b and so take the object as this unit.

Having defined this concept of visibility domain we now consider the mechanism provided by different languages: Modula-3, C++ and Eiffel have different approaches.

3.5.2   Modula-3: visible or hidden

In Modula-3 the default option is that all the fields and methods of a class are visible to any user, but for any given class an opaque type can be created for which visibility can be restricted to selected methods. The rather cumbersome mechanism requires at least two types to be created for each class, an open type containing all the fields and methods and a closed type, available to the users, allowing access only to the selected methods.

This mechanism does offer the possibility of constructing several different interfaces to any given class by limiting the access in different ways. Thus a derived class may need a broader access to its base class than an arbitrary class.

3.5.3 C++: private, protected or public

In C++ the fields and methods are referred to collectively as the members and the visibility rules apply equally to both. The term *accessibility* is used here rather than visibility; there is a significant difference, but we shall not go into the details. The type of visibility is intermediate between those of Modula-3 and Eiffel. A member of a class can be declared with any one of three levels, private, protected or public:

1. A private member is accessible only by the methods of the class in which it is defined. It cannot be accessed from any other class, even a derived class
2. A protected member is accessible only by the methods of the class in which it is defined and the derived classes. This reflects the special status of the derived classes.
3. A public member is accessible by any client user without restriction.

These levels are transmitted by inheritance; thus a public (protected) member of a class A is public (protected) in any derived class of A, but a private member is not visible in any inherited class.

These rules are complemented by three mechanisms concerning visibility:

1. Private inheritance enables a derived class B of A to be constructed for which the inheritance link is not visible outside A; thus the members inherited from A are private in B and there is no inheritance polymorphism (discussed in Chapter 2, section 2.5) between B and A.
2. A class can re-export an inherited member with a different visibility level: for example, a method m that is protected in A

can be made public in a derived class B. With private inheritance this allows specified members of the base class to be made visible.

3. A class A can have **friend** classes and methods which have access to all the members of A. This makes it possible to open a class to authorized users whilst denying access to all others; in effect, it is A that declares which classes and methods are its friends.

3.5.4 Eiffel: explicit export

Of the three languages we are considering Eiffel provides the most precise means for controlling visibility: every class must list the members that it exports, and for each exported member the classes that are allowed to use it can also be listed. A member thus qualified is visible only to the classes stated and to their derived classes; one not qualified in this way is visible to any user.

The same mechanism applies to inherited members: an inherited member can be declared with either the same visibility as in the base class or with a different one.

3.5.5 Problems still to be solved

A variety of considerations of a syntactic nature can lead to a preference for one method for handling visibility rather than another. Whichever method is chosen, it is never easy to manage the combination of visibility, inheritance and polymorphism.

The diversity of syntax hides a complex semantic problem. There is no simple mechanism, because we are not yet able to handle the concept of visibility in a satisfactory way. It is difficult to specify the needs precisely: visibility must be compatible with inheritance, but it must be possible for one class to give a privileged access to another that has no inheritance link, such as with the C++ friend mechanism. A global mechanism, therefore, is necessary, but not sufficient. Some promising work is being done on the concept of *view*: different views of the same class provide different interfaces and users choose the one that best suits their purpose. This has similarities to the Modula-3 mechanism.

This aspect of object-oriented languages is still fluid; we can expect to see solutions to the problems in the reasonably near future.

3.6 SPECIFIC MECHANISMS

3.6.1 Initialization of objects

Initialization is a classical source of problems in languages that manipulate variables or, as in our case, objects. In Pascal, for example, variables that have not been initialized are not identified by the compiler and may cause the program to behave in an arbitrary manner; and even when such identification is possible the programmer must initialize all the variables explicitly, which encumbers the program. The concept of object seems to offer possibilities for improvement here, for one can envisage there being a mechanism that will automatically take charge of the initialization of every new object. Such a mechanism is in fact provided by C++ and by Eiffel.

An Eiffel class can declare a special method to perform this function for all its objects; this must have the predefined name `Create`, and has a special status. The programmer must make an explicit call to this method, and the instruction `o.Create` will invoke the methods of `Create` for the class of the object `o` and for each of its base classes; this ensures that all the components of `o` are initialized correctly. Necessarily, `Create` is not inherited; the compiler generates a version of the method for those classes in which it is not defined, which initializes each field to a default value determined by its type.

In C++ a class can declare what are called **constructors**, special methods carrying the name of the class itself. By declaring a number of different constructors, each with its own list of parameters, different initializations can be made available; a constructor without a parameter list initializes to default values. The compiler calls the relevant constructor automatically when each new object is declared. As in Eiffel, a constructor in a derived class automatically calls that of the base class; in contrast to Eiffel the call of a constructor is made implicitly, thus avoiding unfortunate oversights.

Symmetrically, C++ provides also for the destruction of objects: special methods called **destructors** are called automatically when objects become inaccessible. Thus if an object has been declared as a local variable for a method its destructor will be called when the execution of the method terminates.

Guaranteed destruction of objects is as important as is guaranteed initialization. For example, if a file is represented by an object the destructor will ensure that it is closed when the object becomes inaccessible. Destructors are used most often to destroy dynamic structures contained in objects: thus a class List containing a linked list of objects can ensure the destruction of the elements it contains by defining a destructor.

The definition and use of a constructor and a destructor are illustrated by the following program, for the class Tower. Here we have extended the syntax of our language by adding the keywords constructor and destructor.

```
Tower = class Stack {
   ...
  methods
    constructor (size: integer);
    destructor;
      ...
}

constructor Tower (size: integer) {
  Initialize (size);
}

destructor Tower {
  while top > 0 do Pop ( );
}

{-- example of use
  t: Tower (10);   -- constructor Tower (integer)
    ...
} -- call to destructor of t
```

3.6.2 Genericity

Throughout this chapter we have used the class Stack to represent a stack of integers. If we wished to deal with a stack of other objects we should have to define a new class, whose definition and implementation would probably be not very different from those of Stack. In such a situation it would be helpful if we had some means for defining general types, and genericity, which makes use of parametric polymorphism, is an attractive mechanism. Any class that contains a collection of objects – an array, a list, a tree, etc. – is a good candidate for a generic class: such classes depend very little on the classes of the objects they contain.

In the Stack example genericity enables us to define a generic class GStack, parametrized by the type of its elements:

```
GStack = class (T: class) {
  fields
    stack: array [1 .. N} of T;
    top: integer;
  methods
    procedure Push (val: T);
    procedure Pop ( );
    function Top ( ): T;
}

Stack = class GStack (integer);   -- instantiation
p: Stack;
p.Push (10);
```

The class GStack cannot be used as such; it must be instantiated by giving the type of its elements, integer in the example above. However, classes can be derived from generic classes, and they too will be generic.

Genericity and inheritance are mechanisms by means of which potentially infinite families of classes can be defined. Neither mechanism can be reduced to the other, and a language that provides genericity is certainly more powerful than one that does not. Both Eiffel and C++ allow generic classes to be defined.

3.6.3   Dynamic management of objects

We introduced the concept of an object as a generalization of that of a record as defined in languages such as Pascal. In Pascal and certain other languages objects can be declared whose lifetime is limited by their scope – these are the local variables; but it is possible also to use dynamic variables accessed by means of pointers. This leaves to the programmer the task of destroying the dynamic variables when they are no longer needed, unless a garbage collector is provided which automatically destroys variables when they become inaccessible.

In C++ objects are implemented by means of records and the programmer can use either local objects or pointers to dynamic objects. In the latter case the dynamic allocation and the deletion of unnecessary or inaccessible objects are left to the programmer; constructors and destructors help in these operations but do not make them completely transparent. In contrast, Modula-3 and Eiffel relieve the programmer of these tasks: an object is implemented by a pointer to the record containing the fields and at run time a garbage collector destroys inacessible objects automatically.

Implementation of objects by means of pointers, rather than by records as in C++, has the advantage of simplicity but the disadvantage that at run time indirection is needed to access the fields. This can be costly. Further, the garbage collectors so far available are generally inefficient and are costly in terms of execution time and memory space.

This problem, of course, is not peculiar to object-oriented languages. However, we could hope that the choice of the method of managing objects at run time is not dictated by the choice of language. Modula-3 provides this desired freedom of choice by making it possible to indicate for each class whether the management is to be performed automatically by means of the garbage collector or left as a task for the programmer. C++ too allows the programmer to redefine, for each class, how dynamic objects are to be handled; this makes it possible to take advantage of specific properties of a class so as to manage the memory more efficiently than would be possible with a garbage collector.

3.7   CONCLUSION

The rich possibilities offered by typed object-oriented languages are far from being exhausted. The existing languages are still suffering from their past, inherited from the structured languages. Much research is being done on the type systems used by these languages, revealing the complexity of the problems that arise when we try to combine the concepts of multiple inheritance, genericity, overloading, and so on. The current languages have already demonstrated their strengths: safety for the programmer, ease of maintenance of programs, reuse of code and efficiency of executable code. They are being used more and more by organizations that have to develop complex software such as operating systems, programming environments, graphical user interfaces and simulation.

4

Smalltalk and its derivatives

In this chapter we describe the language Smalltalk and those derived from it. These languages show the features common to all untyped languages, whether interpreted or semi-compiled.

The first version of Smalltalk dates from 1972, inspired by the concepts in Simula and the ideas of Alan Kay of the Xerox PARC laboratory. After some ten years of development and a number of intermediate versions, notably Smalltalk-72 and Smalltalk-76, Smalltalk-80 is the most widely used version, together with the library of classes that goes with it. Accompanying this version are also an operating system and a graphical programming environment, and Xerox have produced machines, Star and Dorado, designed specially for the language. Today Smalltalk is available on UNIX workstations, on Apple Macintosh and on IBM PCs and compatibles.

For the examples in this chapter we shall use a syntax that is close to that of Smalltalk itself, in which comments are signalled by two dashes << -- >> and continue to the end of the line. Every instruction is the **sending of a message**, which can have any of the following forms:

```
receiver msg1
receiver msg2 argument
receiver key1:arg1 key2:arg2 ... keyn:argn
```

The first form is the sending of a unary message, a message with no arguments: for example

```
3 factorial   -- compute 3!
Array new     -- create a new array
```

The second is for binary messages, messages with a single argument. Arithmetical and boolean expressions are given in this form:

```
3 + 4   -- receiver = 3,   msg = +,   argument = 4
a < b   -- receiver = a,   msg = <,   argument = b
```

The third form is for *n*-ary messages, messages with one or more arguments, called keyword messages; each keyword is terminated with a colon << : >> and corresponds to an argument. An example is

```
arr at:3   put: a
```

meaning 'assign the value a to element 3 of the array arr'. Here the receiver is arr, the message is at:put: and the arguments are 3 and a.

The name of a keyword message is the concatenation of its keywords, including the colons; one name can be prefixed to another, and so on, and the name is taken to be the longest sequence of keywords. Parentheses can be used to resolve ambiguities and to enforce a particular order of evaluation. As an example, consider the use of the messages at: and at:put: for accessing the elements of an array:

```
arr at: 3                    -- arr[3]
arr at: 4 put: a             -- arr[4]:= a
arr at: (arr at: 5) put: a   -- arr[arr[5]]:= a
```

The first instruction returns the value of element 3 of the array arr. The second assigns a to element 4. The third assigns a to the element whose index is the value of element 5. The keywords at: put: are not reserved words in Smalltalk, and so are not restricted to accessing arrays, and the array is not a predefined type.

Two other symbols we shall use are << ← >> to denote assignment and << ↑ >> to denote return of a value. We shall use also the concept of *block*, which we define in the next section.

Classes can be defined in Smalltalk by sending messages; this however is cumbersome and instead we shall use a notation that resembles that of Smalltalk's graphical programming environment. With this, classes are declared as follows:

```
class        idClass
superclass   idClass
fields       id1 id2 ... idn
methods
   list of declarations of methods
```

The same format is used to add one or more methods to an existing class, by omitting the lines `superclass` and `fields`. A method is declared as follows:

```
key1:arg1 key2:arg2 ... keyn:argn
  | idvar1 idvar2 ... idvarn |
  body of method
```

The first line is the name of the method – here, a keyword method. The second, optional, allows local variables to be declared. The third gives the body of the method, in Smalltalk written as a sequence of expressions separated by full points.

4.1 EVERYTHING IS AN OBJECT

The basic concepts of Smalltalk can be expressed as the following four axioms.

1. Every entity is an object.
2. Every object is an instance of a class.
3. Every class is a subclass of another class.
4. Every object is activated by the receipt of a message.

Axioms 2 and 3 define the concepts of instantiation and inheritance respectively, and it is fundamental to the understanding of Smalltalk to distinguish clearly between the two types of link to which these correspond: the `is-an-instance-of` of instantiation and the `is-a-subclass-of` of inheritance.

It follows from Axioms 1 and 2 that any class, being an entity of the system, is an object; as an object it must be an instance of a class, which we call its *metaclass*. The concept of metaclass is fundamental in Smalltalk; we return to this later.

The only predefined entities in Smalltalk are:

1. the integers, defined in the class `Integer`;
2. the class `Object`, the only exception to Axiom 3: `Object` is not a subclass of any class;
3. the class `Block`, defined below;
4. the metaclass `Class`.

The only control structure is the sending of a message to an object: in particular, conditional operations, loops and similar structures are handled through the medium of blocks. A block is an instance of the class `Block`; it contains a list of executable Smalltalk expressions separated by full points, and, optionally, a list of parameters. A block is evaluated by sending the unary message `value`.

Blocks are written enclosed in square brackets:

```
incr ← [n ← n+1].
incr value.          -- add 1 to n
```

Blocks may be compared to unnamed procedures which can be evaluated by sending the message value, or to the lambda expressions of Lisp. A block may have parameters, in which case its text starts with the list of names of these, separated by colons, and this list is separated from the body of the block by a vertical bar. The message `value:` takes as argument the value of the actual parameter. We shall use only blocks with a single parameter, for example:

```
add ← [:x | n ← n + x]. -- parameter = x
add value: 10.           -- add 10 to n
```

Thus the language is reduced to the bare minimum. We may compare it to Lisp: like Lisp, Smalltalk is provided with an environment which relieves the programmer of the need to recreate every structure for every new program. This environment is a set of classes for general use, such as booleans, arrays, character strings, etc., supplemented in Smalltalk by classes which enable interactive graphics applications to be constructed.

4.2   CLASSES, INSTANCES, MESSAGES

By Axiom 2, every object is an instance of a class: we must make clear what are these objects and these classes. An object contains a state, held in a set of fields (called **instance variables** in Smalltalk) which are strictly private and are accessible only from the object. An object can be manipulated only by means of messages sent to it, to which it responds by activating methods (Axiom 4). The methods are held, not in the object but in the class of which it is an instance; the instantiation link that ties the object to the class is therefore of crucial importance, since it enables the correct method to be found, and so activated when the message is received.

In the class the methods are held in the **dictionary of methods** together with their bodies. A class contains also the list of field names of its instances, which enables it to create new instances – thus a class is an object generator. Creation of an object, or instantiation, is brought about by sending the message New to the class, to which the class, acting as an object responds by creating the object as shown in Figure 4.1.

We can summarize as follows.

1. An object contains a set of fields;
2. A class contains the descriptions of the fields of its instances and the dictionary of the methods that can be executed by these instances;
3. An object is created by sending the message New to its class.

The link between the message sent to an object and the method to be activated is the name of the method: the object searches the dictionary in its class for a method of that name and if such a method is found it is executed in the context of the receiving object. The body of the method is given access to the fields of the object, which, as we have said, are private to the object.

If a method of the required name is not found in the dictionary the error message DoesNotUnderstand: is sent to the object, with the name of the message as argument. Provided that the

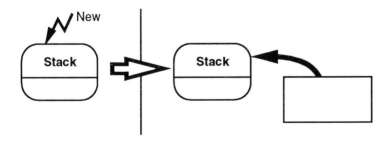

Figure 4.1 Instantiation of an object in Smalltalk.

class has a method with the name `DoesNotUnderstand` the object then has the possibility of recovering from the error; if not, a fatal run-time error is signalled.

The mechanism for responding to a message is dynamic and is not typed; it depends only on the class of the receiver object, which determines which dictionary is to be searched for the method. The same message, therefore, can cause different methods to be executed, according to the class of the receiver. The class of the arguments is not considered; if we want to ensure that a particular argument of the message belongs to a particular class we must insert whatever tests are necessary; since classes are objects, this is a matter of testing whether or not the class of an object is equal to a given class.

The dynamic nature of the mechanism allows the dictionary of methods to be modified during execution, with the effect that a previously rejected message may become comprehensible. Since a method is defined by sending a message, one method may define others, just as a Lisp function may define other functions.

4.2.1 Creating a class

As an example we now show how the class `Stack` is implemented in Smalltalk. We use the class `Array` of the Smalltalk environment and two messages:

`at:`   to access an element of an array
`at:put:` to change the value of an element of an array

```
class        Stack
superclass   Object
fields       stack top
methods
  Initialize
    stack ← Array New.
    top   ← 0
  Push: anObject
    top ← top + 1.
    stack at:top put: anObject.
  Pop
    top ← top - 1.
  Top
    ↑ stack at:top.
```

The class Stack inherits from Object, which is a predefined class in Smalltalk. A stack has two fields, an array that represents the stack and the index in this array of the stack top.

A method is activated in response to a message sent to an object. Within the body of the method reference can be made to the arguments of the message and to the names of the fields of the object's class; these field names will reference the fields of the receiving object.

We have defined four methods for the class Stack as follows.

1. Initialize, which initializes the fields; the field stack receives an object from the class Array, and top is initialized to 0;
2. Push takes as argument an object (the object to be put on the stack). No check is made on the class of the object, so objects of different classes can be stacked – our stack is heterogeneous;
3. Pop removes the element at the stack top;
4. Top returns the current value of the top.

The stack so defined is not very secure, for there is no check in either Pop or Top for the possibility of the stack being empty. We leave the addition of the necessary tests until after we have shown how to implement conditional expressions.

All we need to do in order to use this class Stack is to create an instance and send it messages:

```
mystack ← Stack New.      -- instantiation
mystack initialize.
mystack Push: 10.
mystack Push: 15.
mystack Pop.
s ← mystack Top.          -- s contains 10
o ← AClass New.           -- instantiate an object
mystack Push: o.
mystack Push: mystack. -- !!
```

The last instruction, strange as it may seem, is perfectly legal, since any object whatever can be stacked.

4.3   INHERITANCE

Axiom 3 states that every class is a subclass of some other class: a single exception is allowed, the class Object, which is not a subclass of any class. This axiom determines the inheritance tree which expresses the links between the classes; Object is the root of this tree, meaning that every class is a subclass of Object, directly or indirectly.

Inheritance enables us to define one class from another, keeping the properties of the starting class. A subclass can enrich an existing class by adding new fields and methods; it can also change the behaviour of the base class by redefining its methods.

Inheritance requires the search process described in the previous section to be modified. When a message is received by an object the latter first searches the dictionary of methods of its class for the name of the method contained in the message; if it does not find the required method there it continues with the base class, and so on until either it finds the method or reaches the root, Object.

If this process fails to find a method of the name of the message, the message DoesNotUnderstand: is sent to the receiver, together with the name of the message as argument.

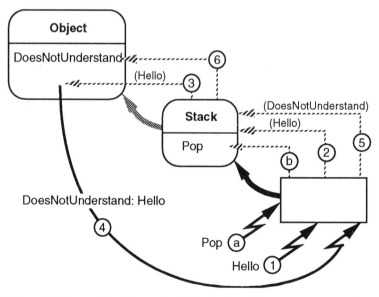

Figure 4.2 Invocation of a method. The hachured arrows represent the search for the method. The message Pop succeeds but Hello fails.

The search for a method DoesNotUnderstand: follows the same route: first the class of the object is searched, then the successive base classes until Object is reached, which defines DoesNotUnderstand:; thus one can be certain that this second search will not fail as shown in Figure 4.2. This way of handling messages that are not understood allows any class to redefine DoesNotUnderstand: and to provide a means of recovery from the error, without any need to add anything to the language such as the concept of 'exception'.

4.3.1 Defining a subclass

We now define class HStack, a subclass of Stack such that all the elements must be of the same class – a homogeneous stack, in fact. For this we add a field to hold the class of the objects to be stacked, and a means for assigning a value to this field. We must then redefine Push to include a check on the class of any object that is to be stacked.

We need to provide a conditional statement; this will have the form

```
bool ifTrue: [block IfTrue] ifFalse: [block IfFalse]
```

The message ifTrue: ifFalse: is sent to an object of class Boolean. The arguments of this message are two blocks, which give respectively the actions to be taken according to whether the object is true or false; we explain later how the class Boolean and control structures such as this are defined.

We can now define the class HStack:

```
class       HStack
superclass  Stack
fields      class
methods
  Class: aClass
     class ← aClass.
     self Initialize.
  Push: anObject
     anObject Class = class
       ifTrue: [super Push: anObject]
       ifFalse: ["Push: class error" Write].
```

The method `Class:` enables us to define the class of the objects that may be put on the stack; it assigns the field `class` and executes `self Initialize`. The method `Push:` is redefined so as to test the class of any object submitted for putting on the stack; for this it uses the method `Class`, defined in the class `Object`, which returns the class of its receiver. The receiver of the message `ifTrue:ifFalse:` is the result of the expression `anObject Class = class`. This consists of the sending of the unary message `Class` to `anObject`. The result is then compared with the field `class` by means of the binary message `=`. If this expression is true, that is, if the object is of the required class, the block to be executed is `super Push`; if false, meaning that the object is not of this class, an error is signalled by sending the message `Write` to a string of characters.

We now define `self` (used in `Class`) and `super` (used in `Push`).

Self and super (Figure 4.3)

As we have emphasized, the body of a method is executed in the context of the object which receives the message, and the fields

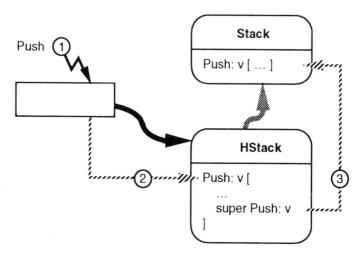

Figure 4.3 The pseudovariables `self` and `super`.

of the object are accessible directly from within this body. If however we wish to send a message to the receiver itself we must have some means of naming the latter, and for this we use the pseudovariable `self`, to mean the receiver of the method currently being executed. Thus in the method `Class:` above, the message `Initialize` is sent to the receiver itself of the message (`self`).

When we wish to redefine a method in a subclass we shall in general need to use the method of the same name in the base class; for this we use another pseudovariable, `super`, to mean the receiving object considered as an instance of the base class – or superclass, hence the name. This is illustrated above by the method `Push:`, which applies the test to find if the object is of the right class and, if it is, puts it on the stack. The message `Push:` is sent to `super`, not to `self`, to ensure that the search for this name starts in the superclass of the receiver and not, as would be the case normally, in its own class. Sending the message to `self` would have the unwanted effect of starting a recursive call.

In practice, `super` is used only in the body of a redefined method, as in this example. This is in fact the only situation in which a call of the same method in the base class is justified; use of `super` in any other context would breach the class boundaries of the receiving object.

4.3.2 Implementing the sending of the message

A consequence of inheritance and the possibility of dynamic modification of the dictionaries of methods is that at run time the sending of a message initiates a search for the relevant method through a chain of superclasses. Sending a message is therefore a very costly operation.

In most cases this cost can be greatly reduced, and performance therefore greatly improved, by the use of a **cache**. This depends on the fact that the inheritance tree and the dictionaries themselves remain largely unaffected, compared to the number of messages sent. Each entry to the cache is a couple

```
<name of class, message name>
```

and for each entry the cache contains the result of the search for the message in the class and its superclasses. When a message is sent the cache is searched for an entry corresponding to the class of the object receiving the message and the message name. If such an entry is found there is no need for any further search; if not, the normal search of the dictionaries is performed and the result entered in the cache. It is found that a 98% 'hit rate' in the cache is easily achieved, which implies a considerable improvement in performance.

The cache must be cleared whenever any change is made to the inheritance tree or to a message dictionary, therefore adding a class or a method will incur a high cost. To combat this, methods have been developed to make it possible to avoid the need for clearing the entire cache after every such change.

4.4   CONTROL STRUCTURES

A special feature of Smalltalk is that it has no predefined control structures; instead, such structures are defined in terms of classes and methods, using the predefined class of blocks, as we now show.

4.4.1   Booleans and the conditional

Consider again the conditional, which we introduced in Section 4.3.1. The receiver of the message `ifTrue:ifFalse:` is a boolean; according to its value, one of the two blocks that are the arguments of the message is executed. This is achieved by defining three classes and two objects:

1. the class `Boolean`, of which there are no instances;
2. the class `True`, a subclass of `Boolean`, of which there is a single instance, the object `true`;
3. the class `False`, a subclass of `Boolean`, of which there is a single instance, the object `false`.

The receiver of `ifTrue:ifFalse:` can be either the object `true` or the object `false`; thus the evaluation of the statement `3 < 4` will return the object `true`, that of the statement `1 = 0` will return the object `false`. This message, therefore, need be defined only in the classes `True`, `False`.

```
class      True
superclass Boolean
fields
methods
  ifTrue:blockTrue ifFalse:blockFalse
    ↑blockTrue value.
class      False
superclass Boolean
fields
methods
  ifTrue:blockTrue ifFalse:blockFalse
    ↑blockFalse value.
```

If the object `true` receives a message `ifTrue:ifFalse:` it returns the value of the first argument; if `false`, that of the second. Method dispatching has therefore enabled us to reproduce conditional behaviour.

The process can be used to define other messages, for example the operators of logic:

```
class      True
methods
  not
      ↑false.
  or: aBool
      ↑true.
  and: aBool
      ↑aBool.

class      False
methods
  not
      ↑true.
  or: aBool
      ↑aBool.
  and: aBool
      ↑false.
```

Given these definitions of the methods `not`, `or:`, `and:` in the classes `True`, `False` respectively we can easily implement the truth tables for these operators. Figure 4.4 illustrates the evaluation of a boolean expression involving them.

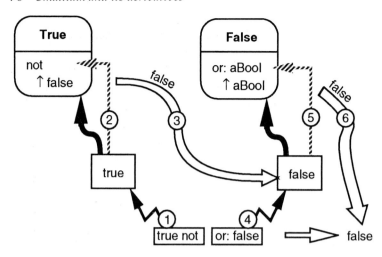

Figure 4.4 Evaluation of the expression (true not) or: false.

So far we have not made any use of the class Boolean, and in fact True and False could just as well have been inherited from Object. We now show how Boolean can be used to share methods between the classes True and False.

```
class       Boolean
superclass  Object
fields
methods
   ifTrue: aBlock
           ↑self ifTrue: aBlock ifFalse: [ ].
   ifFalse: aBlock
           ↑self ifTrue:[ ] ifFalse: aBlock.
      xor: aBool
           ↑(self or: aBool)
           and: ((self and: aBool) not).
```

In the class Boolean we have defined two conditionals, ifTrue: and ifFalse:, which correspond to the conditional ifTrue:ifFalse: when one of the blocks is omitted. As Figure 4.5 shows, it is not necessary to define these conditionals in the classes True and False. Similarly, the exclusive or

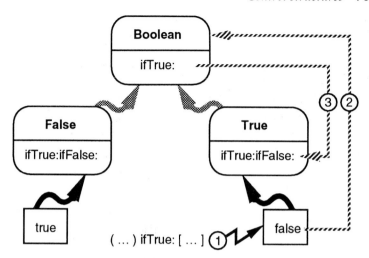

Figure 4.5 Evaluation of conditionals.

operator `xor` is defined in terms of the elementary operators `and:`, `or:`, `not`, by means of the expression

```
a xor b = (a or b) and not (a and b)
```

4.4.2 Blocks and loops

Loop structures need to be defined, not in the class `Boolean`, but in the class `Block`. Consider first the while loop:

```
class           Block
methods
  whileTrue: body.
      (self value) ifTrue: [body value. self
whileTrue: body].
```

The message `whileTrue` is used as follows:

```
[x < 10] whileTrue: [s ← s + x x ← x - 1]
```

The receiver of the message is a block which, as the implementation shows, is evaluated at each cycle through the loop; if it is true the body of the loop is evaluated and the message whileTrue is sent to the receiver, thus continuing the iteration.

As is always the case in Smalltalk, there is no check on types; so there is nothing to prevent us from writing

```
[10] whileTrue: [ ... ].
```

or

```
"Hello" whileTrue: [ ... ].
```

In the first case the evaluation of the receiver block will return the value 10, which belongs to the class Integer; the method ifTrue: has not been defined for this class, so an error will be signalled and the execution halted. In the second case the receiver is a string of characters which cannot respond to value: so again an error will be signalled. But if these methods had been defined for these classes it could have been possible for the execution to continue.

The other kind of controlled structure we are going to look at is *iteration*, execution of the body of a loop (a block) a stated number of times. The equivalent of the Pascal iterative loop is achieved with the aid of a new class Interval, containing two integers defining the lower and upper bounds respectively of the interval over which the iteration is to be performed. The actual iteration is performed by a new method repeat, sent to the interval.

```
class       Interval
superclass  Object
fields      inf sup
methods
  Inf:i Sup:s
    inf ← i. sup ← s.
  repeat:body
    |i|
    i ← inf.
    [i < sup] whileTrue:
    [body value:i.
    i ← i + 1].
```

The method Inf:Sup: sets the bounds of the Interval, repeat: introduces the local variable i to act as a counter for the loop and uses the message whileTrue to control the iteration. An iteration is performed as follows.

```
bounds ← Interval New.
bounds Inf:10 Sup:20.
s ← 0.
bounds repeat [:x | s ← s + x].
s Write.                    -- s = 165
```

The example computes the sum (165) of the numbers from 10 to 20.

To simplify the writing of an iteration we add a message to: to the predefined class Integer:

```
class Integer
methods
  to:val
  ↑(Interval new) Inf:self Sup:val.
    -- instantiation of new Interval
```

This enables us to create an interval by sending the message to: to an integer, with an integer as argument; the lower bound of the interval is then the receiver of this message and the upper bound is the argument. Thus the above example can be written

```
s ← 0.
(10 to: 20) repeat [:x | s ← s + x].
s Write.
```

The expression 10 to: 20 returns an interval to which the iteration message repeat: is sent.

Iteration can be used with many classes. Smalltalk provides a large number of container classes for storing objects such as arrays, lists, sets, dictionaries, etc. The majority of these classes have methods that enable iteration over their elements to be performed. As an example, iteration for the class Stack is made possible by adding a method repeat: which evaluates a given block for each successive element of a stack:

```
class        Stack
methods
  repeat: aBlock
    (1 to: top) repeat:
      [ :i | aBlock value: (stack at: i)].
```

Here we have used the message to: to create an interval that represents the set of indices currently valid in the stack, and the method `repeat` to iterate over this interval; for each element of the stack the argument `aBlock` is evaluated with the element as argument.

To print out the contents of the stack all we need to write is:

```
stack ← Stack New.
stack Initialize.
  -- put elements on the stack ...
stack repeat: [:e | e Write].
```

We have used the method `repeat:` of the class `Interval`, to define a method `repeat:` for the class `Stack`; thus we have used the *ad hoc* polymorphism that is inherent in all object-oriented languages. Similarly we could define for the class `Object` itself a method for printing the contents of an object:

```
class Object
methods
  WriteContent
    self repeat:[:e | e Write].
```

Then any object that can respond to a message `repeat:` could execute `WriteContents`, thus:

```
(10 to: 20) WriteContents.  -- writes integers
                               from 10 to 20
stack ← Stack New.
stack Initialize
stack Push: 5.
stack Push: 10.
stack WriteContents.  -- writes 5,10
```

We have defined iteration – the message `repeat:` – for the class `Stack` in terms of iteration over an interval; iteration is defined in terms of repetition of a block - `whileTrue:` – which in turn is defined recursively in terms of the conditional `ifTrue:`. Finally, this conditional is defined in terms of the general conditional `ifTrue:ifFalse:`, itself defined for the classes `True` and `False`. This illustrates the power and flexibility of Smalltalk, resulting from its extensive use of dynamic binding: by simply adding methods to a class, as with `repeat:` added to `Stack`, we can endow instances of the class with new capabilities, as `WriteContents` here. Because of this Smalltalk provides an ideal environment for modelling and prototyping applications. On the other hand, its absence of typing, with the consequential lack of assurance that a program will not generate messages that cannot be understood, is often an obstacle to its use for the final version of an application.

4.5 METACLASSES

The first axiom of Smalltalk is that everything is an object, and the second that every object is an instance of a class; it follows that every class is an object and therefore belongs to a class – known as a **metaclass**. This feature underlies many interesting and important possibilities in Smalltalk.

The metaclass concept enables instantiation to be realized by the sending of a message. The message New sent to a class returns an instance of that class; and since it has been sent to a class, it is the metaclass that must be searched for the corresponding method as shown in Figure 4.6.

Metaclasses are not used only for instantiation. A class contains the definition of its instances, that is, the list of names of its fields and the dictionary of its methods. Thus a class can be sent messages in order to find if a particular method is defined,

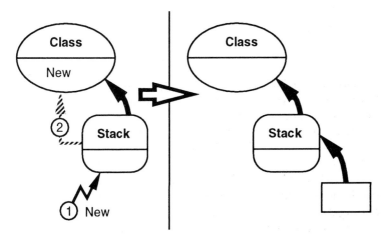

Figure 4.6 Creation of an object: use of the metaclass.

to modify the method dictionary and to define new subclasses. For example, `Understands:` enables us to find whether or not a class can respond to a message whose name is passed as an argument; `Superclass` returns the receiver's base class; and `IsSubclassOf:` enables us to test whether or not the receiver class is derived from the class whose name is passed as an argument. The following are examples of the use of these messages.

```
Stack Understands: "Push:".       -- true
Stack Understands: "IfTrue:".      -- false
True Superclass.                   -- Boolean
True IsSubclassOf: "Stack".        -- false
HStack IsSubclassOf: "Object".     -- true
```

The bodies of the methods corresponding to these messages are held in the dictionaries of the receivers' metaclasses; this is shown by the following examples.

```
Stack Understands: "New".             -- false
(Stack Class): Understands: "New". -- true
```

Several models of metaclasses have been experimented with in Smalltalk. The simplest had a single metaclass for the whole system, called `Class`; this of course made it impossible to distinguish metaclasses of different classes, which in the later versions of the language was felt to be too limiting. The Smalltalk-80 model defines a metaclass for each different class, each class is the sole instance of its metaclass and the inheritance hierarchy of metaclasses is the same as that of the classes. The metaclasses are transparent to the user since they are created automatically by the method for defining a class.

The naming convention is that the metaclass of class `X` is `XClass`, so that the metaclass of `Object` is `ObjectClass` and of `Stack` is `StackClass`. Since `Stack` inherits from `Object`, `StackClass` inherits from `ObjectClass`. All the metaclasses inherit from `Class`, which in turn inherits from `Object`.

The metaclass mechanism leads to an infinite regress: a metaclass is itself an object and must therefore belong to a class, which must have a metaclass.... As with the inheritance hierarchy, this is artificially cut short by means of a loop in the chain of metaclasses; in Smalltalk-80 all the metaclasses are

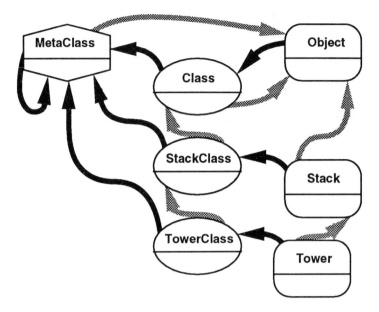

Figure 4.7 The model of metaclasses in Smalltalk-80.

made to inherit from the class `Class` and are instances of the single `Metaclass` as shown in Figure 4.7. Whilst this trick is in itself of little significance for the programmer, it ensures **metacircularity** for the language, that is, the ability of the language to describe itself: metaclasses make it possible to write an interpreter for Smalltalk in Smalltalk.

4.5.1 Importance of metaclasses for the programmer

For the programmer, metaclasses enable, on the one hand, class methods to be defined and on the other, fields to be shared by all the instances of a class.

Class methods are methods defined in a metaclass and used when messages are sent to a class. The commonest uses of class methods are the redefinition of the instantiation method `New` and the definition of other instantiation methods involving parameters; it becomes possible to approximate the constructors provided by certain typed object-oriented languages – see Chapter 3, section 3.6.

Consider again the class `Stack`, for which we have defined the method `Initialize` to enable us to instantiate and initialize the fields of a stack. When using this class we create instances by means of `New` and must be sure to initialize each stack thus created:

```
stack ← Stack New.
stack Initialize.
```

If we forget this initialization the stack cannot work as we intend. It would be safer to build in a means for ensuring that instantiation is always followed by initialization. This can be done by redefining `New` as follows.

```
class     StackClass     -- Stack's metaclass
methods
  New
    |stack|
    stack ← super New.
    stack Initialize.
    ↑stack.
```

The method is defined in the metaclass of `Stack` since the receiver of `New` is the class `Stack`. It first instantiates the stack by sending the message *New* to *super*. This considers the receiver of the message (the class stack) as an instance of *ObjectClass*, the superclass of *StackClass*. As a result it invokes the method *New* defined for all objects in the metaclass *Class*. The resulting stack is then initialized: the message `Initialize` is sent to the stack, invoking the method `Initialize` of the class `Stack`. Finally the initialized stack is returned.

The body of this method could be condensed to

```
↑super New Initialize.
```

The fields of the object `stack` cannot be accessed from within the body of the method; they can be initialized only by means of a message sent to the stack.

The redefining of `New` in this way means that any class which inherits from `Stack` will use the redefined method, because inheritance between classes parallels that between metaclasses. Instantiation of the class `HStack`, for example, ensures its initialization, as shown in Figure 4.8.

Metaclasses also enable methods for initialization with parameters to be defined. The following example shows how the size of a stack can be set at the time of its creation.

```
class       Stack
methods
  Initialize: size
     stack ← Array New: size.
     top ← 0.
class       StackClass
methods
  New: size
     ↑super New Initialize: size.
```

Here we have added to the class `Stack` a method `Initialize:` which takes the size of the stack as argument. This argument is given to the method `New:` of the class `Array`. The method `New:` is then defined for the metaclass of `Stack`, which method instantiates a stack and initializes it with the given size; this method `New:` is a binary method (it has a single parameter) and must not be confused with the unary method `New` (with no parameter) used up to the present.

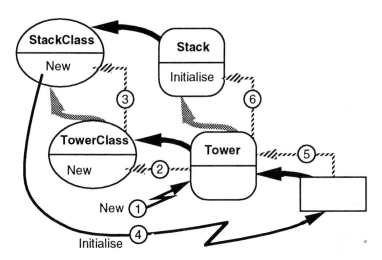

Figure 4.8 Inheritance of class methods.

Having defined this *class method,* we can now use it as follows:

```
stack ← Stack New: 100.
stack Push: 10.
```

The same mechanism could be used to define a method for the class HStack which would use as parameter the class of the objects that are to be put on the homogeneous stack.

4.5.2   Class variables

The other use of metaclasses is in adding new fields to a class; these fields are accessible to all instances of the class (every instance knows to which class it belongs) and play the role of global variables of the class. They are called **class variables**.

To illustrate this, let us create a class of objects, each of whose instances bears a unique number. The metaclass for this class will have a field which is incremented at each instantiation.

```
class       Demo
superclass  Object
fields      number
methods
  Initialize: n
    number ← n.
  Number
    ↑number.

class       DemoClass      -- Demo's metaclass
fields      nb
methods
  New
    nb ← nb + 1.
    ↑(super New) Initialize:nb.
```

The class Demo has a field number holding the number that is unique to the instance, a method for instantiation and a method for returning the number of the object. We add to the metaclass of Demo a class variable nb and redefine the method

New to increment this variable, instantiate the object and initialize number with the incremented value of nb.

4.6 DERIVATIVES OF SMALLTALK

Smalltalk was influenced by Lisp and has given rise to a family of object-oriented languages that have been implemented on top of Lisp. Implementation of such languages in Lisp has proved relatively easy, and has provided a convenient field for experimenting with new concepts.

One of the oldest object-oriented extensions to Lisp is Flavors, the language in which the operating system of the Symbolics machine was written in the early 1980s. More recently, CLOS (Common Lisp Object System) has looked at Flavors again and extended it, with the aim of defining a norm for object-oriented Lisp. The languages Ceyx and ObjVLisp represent the French school: Ceyx was developed by Jean-Marie Hullot around 1985, on top of Le_Lisp, whilst the slightly earlier ObjVLisp was produced by Pierre Cointe, starting from VLisp, a dialect of Lisp due to Patrick Greussay of the University of Vincennes.

All these languages are extensions of Lisp; that is, programs written in them use Lisp* functions; the result is not always very convincing, since the functional style of Lisp differs rather radically from the style of an object-oriented language.

In general, the languages provide three basic functions: creation of a new class, creation of an instance of a class and sending a message to an object; when a class is created its inheritance (simple or multiple) can be specified, together with the variables of its instances, its methods and possibly its metaclass. The system will usually be able to generate automatically the functions for accessing the instance variables: these variables are held in a list associated with the atom that represents the object, and can be accessed only by means of a function. This device, however, is practically transparent to the user, as the following example shows.

---

*Some of the elementary concepts of Lisp are used in the examples below; we hope this will not deter the reader who is not very familiar with the language.

```
(def-class Stack (Object)    -- class, superclass
   (stack top))              -- instance variables
(def-method
   (Push Stack)(object)      -- method,  class,
                                  arguments
   (setq top (+ top 1).
   (send 'put stack top object))
```

The syntax of this example was suggested by Flavors. def-class defines a new class, def-method a new method for an existing class. The body of the method Push consists of two expressions: assignment (setq in Lisp) of the field top, and the sending of the message put to the field stack. This message causes the object passed as the second argument to be placed in the element passed as the first argument. The sending of a message is a function, invoked as follows:

```
(send 'message receiver arg1 arg2 ... argn)
```

The syntax can be brought closer to that of Smalltalk by transforming every object into a function, as certain languages do; the sending of a message is then written

```
(receiver message arg1 arg2 ... argn)
```

Creation of a stack and putting an element on it are done as follows:

```
(setq mystack (instantiate 'Stack))
(mystack 'Initialize)
(mystack 'Push 10)
```

The function instantiate causes a class to be instantiated.
   The method Initialize is defined as follows:

```
(def-method
   (Initialize Stack) ( ) -- method, class, arguments
   (setq stack (instantiate 'Array))
   (setq top 0))
```

The advantage of using Lisp as the basis for these languages is that this makes available a considerable programming environment, already developed, that simplifies the implementation of the mechanisms for manipulating objects. Further, the flexibility of Lisp makes it easy to experiment with new functions and to extend the object-oriented model.

4.6.1 'Daemons' in Flavors

Flavors provides sophisticated mechanisms for handling multiple inheritance. We have seen (Chapter 2, section 2.4) that conflicts can arise when a method is defined with the same name in different classes: Flavors enables the programmer to determine the order in which the graph of superclasses is to be traversed, so as to find the right method to be invoked. Further, it allows us to combine a set of methods of the same name, that is, to invoke them one after the other. And finally, it enables us to define **daemons**.

Daemons are special methods associated with ordinary methods. When an ordinary method is invoked all the daemons associated with it in that class and its superclasses are invoked also, in an order that can be laid down by the programmer. Thus to trace the invocations of the message Push we need only add the following daemon:

```
(def-daemon
   (Push Stack) (object)   -- method, class, arguments
   (print "Pushing" object))
```

The daemon will be called even if we redefine Push in a subclass of Stack. The combination of methods and daemons is very powerful, and for that very reason is difficult to handle: the sending of a message to an object can trigger a number of actions, the reasons for which can be difficult to trace. Similarly, a local change to the system, such as the addition or removal of a daemon, can have effects that soon get out of control. Experienced Lisp programmers become adept at exploiting these effects, and as a result find these languages offer even more scope for experiment.

4.6.2 The metaclasses of ObjVLisp

We end this review of the languages derived from Lisp with a look at ObjVLisp and the model of its metaclasses. This model does in fact provide what can be regarded as both the simplest and the most open-ended of metaclass models.

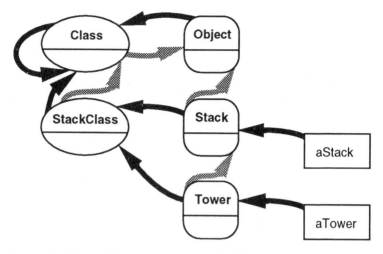

Figure 4.9 The model of metaclasses in ObjVLisp.

Class and Object are the two primitive classes; Object is an instance of Class and Class is a subclass of Object. Object has no superclass and Class is its own instance. Object is the root of the inheritance tree, Class is the root of the instantiation tree; thus every class inherits directly from Object and is an instance either of Class or of a class derived from Class.

This last consequence corresponds to the creation of metaclasses, without the constraints imposed by Smalltalk-80. In Figure 4.9 Stack and Tower have the same metaclass, whereas in Smalltalk-80 each would have its own; here it is useful to have only one metaclass, since the same method of instantiation covers both classes. On the other hand, the Smalltalk model enables the classes to be made transparent to the user, because of the bijection between classes and metaclasses, and this is not the case in ObjVLisp.

4.7 CONCLUSION

Without doubt, the success of the object-oriented model is due to Smalltalk. The language was validated very quickly by the construction of large applications, in particular its programming environment; and the object-oriented extensions to Lisp have made it easier to experiment with such languages and so to gain a better understanding of their mechanisms.

The power of Smalltalk is also its main weakness: with dynamic binding but no typing it is not possible to ensure that a program is correct before execution, not even after; and safety is not helped by the absence of any mechanism for controlling access – every method is accessible to everyone. Some extensions have successfully introduced declaration of the classes of arguments and of local variables; whilst in CLOS the types of the arguments of the methods must be declared. In neither case is there any significant loss in functionality, and indeed in CLOS the typing enables generic methods to be defined, thus increasing the expressive power of the language.

The other weakness of Smalltalk, common to interpreted languages in general, is slow execution. Here too, however, much work has been done on the problem, and some spectacular improvements have been achieved: it has even been found that in certain applications the difference in performance between Smalltalk and a compiled, typed object-oriented language can be made insignificant. But in others the difference remains unacceptable, which simply confirms the view that there is no universal language. Smalltalk remains an especially valuable language for investigating the concepts of object-orientation and also for developing prototypes; and in certain cases it can be valuable for constructing the final applications.

5

Prototypes and actors

This chapter describes two important variations on the basic concepts of object-oriented languages. In one, *prototype-based languages*, the distinction between classes and instances is removed by the introduction of the concept of a prototype object, which replaces inheritance by delegation. In the other, *actor languages*, the concept of sending a message is generalized so as to be adapted to parallel programming: the sending of a message is then not the invocation of a method but a request made to an object.

5.1 PROTOTYPE-BASED LANGUAGES

All the object-oriented languages that we have described so far are based on the concepts of class, instance and inheritance. These three concepts give rise to two relations between the entities of the language: that of instantiation between an object and its class, and that of inheritance between a class and its base class. These concepts and relations characterize the classical object-oriented languages which, to distinguish them from the prototype-based languages, we shall call the **class-based languages**.

The first work on prototype-based languages dates from 1986, with Henry Lieberman at MIT, who at the same time also worked on actor languages. This chapter is based on the language Self, created in 1987, and later developed by David Ungar and Randall Smith at Stanford University; it represents the most advanced state of languages of this type.

5.1.1 Prototypes and cloning

As we have indicated, in a prototype-based language there is no distinction between classes and instances: every object is a prototype and can serve as a model for the creation of further objects. The operation which enables a new object to be created from a prototype is called **cloning**, and consists of copying the object cloned.

In a prototype there is no distinction between state and behaviour; fields and methods are not distinguished, and the two are referred to indifferently as **slots**. To get the value of a field x a prototype sends to itself the message x. To modify this field it sends the message x:, with the new value as argument.

A prototype is declared as a list of couples {name of slot/value}, in braces as shown. A field has an expression as value, whilst a method has a block (in square brackets as in Smalltalk). Thus a prototype stack will be defined as follows.

```
Stack  ←  {
    stack              Array clone.
    top                0.
    Push: anObject     [top: (top + 1).
                        stack at : top put: anObject].
    Pop                [top: (top - 1)].
    Top                [↑stack at: top].
}
```

The slots stack, top are fields, with values corresponding to the initial values given when the prototype is created. The clone message returns a clone of its receiver; it plays the same role as new in Smalltalk-like languages. Since there is no distinction between a clone and its instances, any object can be cloned. Here Array is a prototype array.

The access messages stack, top and the assignment messages stack:, top: are created implicitly. The other slots are methods. Since all accesses to fields are made by messages, the pseudovariable self is the implied receiver of these messages, so that, for example, the method Pop could be written

```
Pop  [self top: (self top - 1)].
```

In the above example, Stack is a prototype and therefore an object that can be used directly; we shall use it as a model to create and manipulate two stacks, as in Figure 5.1:

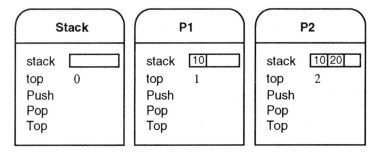

Figure 5.1 The prototype Stack and two clones.

```
pl  ← Stack clone.
pl  Push: 10.
x ← pl top.       -- value of x is 10
p2 ← pl clone.    -- p2 already contains 10
p2  Push: 20.
```

In a class-based language a class contains a *description* of its
instances, whereas in a prototype-based language every object is
an *example* which can be replicated by cloning. As the above
example shows, the mechanism of cloning simplifies the
initialization of objects, all that is required being the correct
initialization of the prototype used as the model. In contrast,
Smalltalk requires the redefinition of the method defined in the
metaclass, and typed object-oriented languages require the
introduction of specific mechanisms such as the constructors in
C++.

5.1.2 Delegation

Cloning is the exact duplication of the prototype in its current
state; this means that the state and the behaviour are copied and
there is no link between the object used as model and that
resulting from the cloning. Figure 5.1 illustrates this, and it
follows that there is no possibility of any form of sharing
between these objects. In a class-based language sharing can be
at either of two levels:

1. by the instantiation link between an object and its class, with all instances of the class having the behaviour described in the class;

2. by the inheritance link between a class and its superclass, the derived class inheriting the description contained in the superclass.

In prototype-based languages a single mechanism, **delegation**, enables objects to share information. An object can delegate to another object, called a parent, a message that it (the delegator) does not understand. In the example of the stack we cause separate stacks to share the methods Push, Pop and Top by putting these into a prototype which will be the parent of all the clone stacks. Whenever one of these messages is sent to one of the clones the latter delegates it to its prototype, in this case protoStack:

```
protoStack ← {
   Push: anObject  [top: (top + 1).
                    stack at: top put: anObject].
   Pop             [top: (top - 1)].
   Top             [↑stack at: top].
```

The prototype is now written as follows:

```
Stack ← {
   parent   protoStack.
   stack    Array clone.
   top      0.
}
```

When a prototype is cloned the objects thus created have the same parent as does their prototype; in our example, the clones of Stack have protoStack as parent. The example of use given above is always valid but, as Figure 5.2 shows, the schema of the objects changes at execution: if a message Push is sent to p1 the latter delegates it to the parent, protoStack.

In this example the couple (Stack, protoStack) plays the role of a class in a class-based language. The instantiation link between an object and its class is achieved by delegation; instantiation is done by cloning, but the class-based method

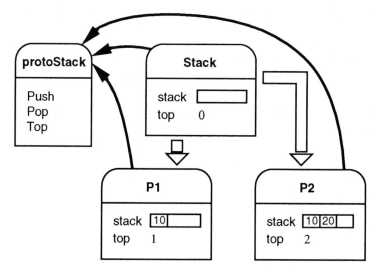

Figure 5.2 Sharing methods with prototypes. The black arrows point to the parent (a field), the light arrows show the cloning operations.

could easily have been simulated by defining in protoStack the method New with the value [↑Stack clone].

This example shows why access to fields has to be made by messages: in the bodies of the methods of protoStack reference is made to fields (top, stack) which are declared in Stack and are therefore unknown to protoStack.

In what follows we shall use the term 'class' to mean a prototype which contains only methods; but it should be kept in mind that a class is not a distinctive concept in prototype-based languages.

5.1.3   Use of delegation to simulate inheritance

To illustrate this we return to the example of the Tower of Hanoi, recalling that a tower is a stack in which some check is applied to the objects presented for stacking. We create a prototype Tower whose parent is the prototype protoTower, which in turn has protoStack as parent.

```
protoTower  ← {
  parent          protoStack.
  Push: anObject  [anObject < Top
          ifTrue: [parent Push: anObject]
          ifFalse: ["Push: object too big" Write].
  ]
}
Tower ← (Stack clone) parent: protoTower.
```

Here we have defined a method `Push:` which requests its parent either to put the candidate object on the stack or to display an error message, according to the size of that object. The prototype `Tower` is created by cloning the existing prototype `Stack`, and changing its parent; the following example and Figure 5.3 illustrates the use of `Tower`.

```
t ← Tower clone.
t Push: 10.
t Push: 20.           -- Push: object too big
```

The example we have just given enables us to draw a parallel between prototype-based and class-based languages. However,

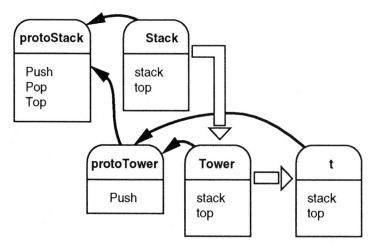

Figure 5.3 Simulating inheritance by delegation. The arrows have the same meaning as in Figure 5.2.

the importance of prototypes lies in the scope they offer for extending the possibilities of class-based languages; they enable us, among other things, to create objects with special properties or with computed fields, and to implement dynamic inheritance. We consider these possibilities in the following paragraphs.

5.1.4 Special behaviour

In the example of the tower, if our application uses only a single tower we can create an object that has the behaviour of a tower without any need to create the corresponding class: all we need to do is to redefine the slot Push: in the object itself, as follows.

```
t ← {
  parent        protoStack.
  stack         Array clone.
  top           0.
  Push: anObject [
    anObject < Top
      ifTrue: [parent Push: anObject]
      ifFalse: {"Push: object too big" write]
  ].
}

t Push: 10.
t Push: 20.  -- Push: object too big
```

This shows how objects can be created so as to have special behaviour; these objects can be cloned, and their clones will have the same behaviour. The Smalltalk objects true and false provide another example. We had to create the classes True and False, each with a unique instance; with prototypes we need only create two prototypes true, false, each containing a version of the method ifTrue: ifFalse:.

The method can be usefully applied in the development of a program, when we may want to monitor the detailed behaviour of a specific object. We can do this by defining a method within that object, as in the following example; here we use the method add:, which adds or replaces slots in an object:

```
p ← Stack clone add: {
    Push: anObject [
        "p Push" Write.
        parent Push: anObject.
    ].
}
```

Every operation of placing an object on the stack p will now cause a message to be displayed. In a class-based language, if a trace is included in the method Push for the class Stack a message will be displayed for every object of that class.

5.1.5   Computed fields

The method of accessing the fields of a prototype by sending a message enables fields to be defined whose values are computed rather than stored in the object. As an illustration, let us define a prototype protoPoint containing methods for manipulating points, and two prototypes of points, Cartesian and Polar, for which their positions are given in Cartesian and polar coordinates respectively.

```
protoPoint ← {
    Write   [x Write." , " Write. y Write].
    +: p    [↑ clone x: (x + px) y: (y + py)].
}
```

The method +: creates a new point whose coordinates are the sum of the coordinates of the receiver and those given as argument.

```
Cartesian ← {
    parent  protoPoint.
        x        0.
        y        0.
}

Polar ← {
    parent  protoPoint.
        ρ        0.
        θ        0.
}
```

However, `Polar` cannot be used as written, since the methods of `protoPoint` use the fields x, y; we can get over this difficulty by simply adding the methods x, y, x: and y: so as to simulate the missing fields, using the relations

$$x = \rho \cos \theta \qquad \rho = \sqrt{(x^2 + y^2)}$$
$$y = \rho \sin \theta \qquad \theta = \arctan(y/x)$$

`Polar` will then appear to have the fields x and y, which are in fact computed from the polar coordinates stored in the object.

```
Polar ← {
    parent      protoPoint.
    ρ           0.
    θ           0.
    x           [↑ρ*(θ cos)].
    y           [↑ρ*(θ sin)].
    x: val      [ρ: (val*val + y*y)sqrt.
                 θ: (y/val)arctan]
    y: val      [ρ: (x*x + val*val)sqrt.
                 θ: (val/x)arctan].
}
```

Similarly, we could add the fields ρ, θ to the prototype `Cartesian`; if both were done we could then always use whichever coordinate system happened to be the more suitable for the particular application.

5.1.6 Dynamic inheritance

Apart from its role as delegator of messages, the parent of a prototype is a slot like all others. The value of the parent slot can be changed after an object has been created: this is dynamic inheritance. For example, having defined `Stack` and `Tower` we can transform a tower into a stack by operating on the slot `parent`.

```
t ← clone Tower.
t Push: 10.
t Push: 20.          -- Push: object too big
t parent: Stack.     -- the tower is changed to a
                        stack
t Push: 20.          -- OK
```

There are many applications for this technique. One is to the situation in which the class of an object cannot be defined completely when the object is created, or may need to be modified during the life of the object; dynamic inheritance enables the class to be defined in more and more detail as further knowledge is acquired. For example, in a graphical system new objects can be created by means of operations between graphical objects, such as intersection and union. If this results in a familiar object such as a rectangle, the parent can be changed so that specialized methods can be used that are more efficient than those that apply to an arbitrary object. Conversely, if an operation on a rectangle transforms it into a more general polygon its parent will need to be changed accordingly.

Dynamic inheritance is equally useful in developing a program: to monitor an object we give it as parent a prototype that traces the operations applied to it. Similarly we could test a new implementation of a class by assigning the new class, at run time, to the parent of some object.

5.1.7 Conclusion

By abolishing the distinction between classes and instances, and unifying the concepts of field and method, prototype-based languages open new prospects for the use of dynamic inheritance with object-oriented languages.

Rather surprisingly, an implementation of a prototype-based language can be more efficient than that of a language such as Smalltalk. This however can only be achieved by using quite complex techniques, in essence holding the results of searches for methods in caches so as to optimize message passing, and compiling different versions of the same method so as to have available the version best suited to the current context.

However, the fact remains that prototype-based languages are untyped and therefore provide no check on the validity of a program before execution. The more feasible it seems to add type declarations to a language such as Smalltalk, the less feasible is this for a prototype-based language. If the type of an object is taken as its parent, no static typing is possible since an object's type can change during its lifetime. Again, the structure of an object can be changed by the addition of slots, so the use of this as the type is equally unfeasible. The conclusion is that in the absence of any means for static verification, the use of a prototype-based language must be restricted to the development of prototype software.

5.2 ACTOR LANGUAGES

Actor languages originated at MIT in the 1970s with Carl Hewitt's language Plasma; in the early 1980s Henry Lieberman, also at MIT, developed ACT1, and shortly after this Akinori Yonezawa at the Tokyo Institute of Technology produced ABCL/1.

The aim of these languages is to provide a model for parallel computing, based on independent, autonomous entities communicating by means of messages. Each entity, called an **actor**, consists of a **state** and a **filter**; the state consists of local variables and references to other actors, the filter is a set of message patterns to which that actor can respond. When an actor receives a message it first checks that there is a corresponding pattern in its filter; if there is, it executes the requisite block of instructions; if not, it passes the message on to another actor, its proxy, which either executes the instructions or delegates further, and so on. This delegation mechanism is similar to that of prototype-based languages, which we have already described and therefore shall not discuss further.

The only actions available to an actor are message sending, creation of new actors and transformation of itself into another actor. Messages are sent asynchronously: an actor does not concern itself with the fate of any message that it sends. Parallelism follows naturally from this asynchronism: the sending actor continues with its own activity while the message is being handled by the receiver. Each actor operates sequentially and has a mailbox in which messages received are stored until it is ready to deal with them.

Creating an actor is simple: any actor can create another, for which it specifies the state, the filter and the proxy. Self-transformation is essentially the same process, except that the newly created actor now replaces the creator – it takes over the latter's mailbox. In the model introduced by Gul Agha an actor can transform itself while still in the process of dealing with a message and therefore can handle several messages in parallel: if when a message arrives it immediately specifies its replacement the latter can then immediately deal with the next message that is waiting. The first actor disappears when it has dealt with its message. Since it is possible to handle messages in parallel it must not be possible to modify the state of an actor; this explains the need to specify a replacement, which will generally be a modified copy of the original.

This asynochronous sending of messages, whilst it brings in parallelism naturally, poses a problem: how is one to send a message and get a result? This is achieved by sending with the message a continuation, a supplementary argument which names the actor to which the receiver of the main message must send the result. Thus an actor can receive the result of a message it sends by naming itself in the continuation but it can name any other which could be better equipped to deal with this result.

As an example, consider three actors: a *reader*, an *evaluator* and a *printer*; the first reads expressions entered on a keyboard, the second evaluates these and the third displays (by printing or on a screen) the results of the evaluations. The reader, having read an expression, sends it as a message to the evaluator with the name of the printer as continuation; and the evaluator, having evaluated the expression, sends the result to the printer. In the

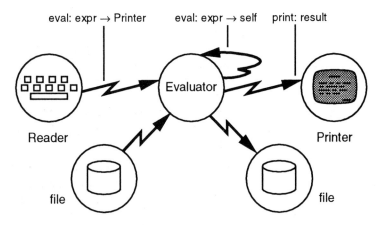

Figure 5.4 Sending messages with continuations.

traditional model the reader would ask the evaluator to evaluate the expression, would receive the result and would then send this to the printer.

For this example it might seem that the continuation serves no purpose, since the evaluator could be instructed to send its results to the printer in every case. But the addition of the continuation enables the evaluator to break a complex expression into a number of subexpressions and send these to itself for evaluation, naming itself as the continuation. Another actor, reading from a file, could send messages to the evaluator with, as continuation, an actor that writes the results in an output file. This is illustrated in Figure 5.4.

5.2.1 Programming with actors

For the examples here we use a syntax adapted from that used for prototypes. An actor is described by its name, possibly followed by its state and its filter. The filter is expressed as a set of couples <message pattern/action>, where a pattern is the name of a message together with arguments, and possibly a continuation indicated by an arrow, '→'. Creation of actors and sending of messages are written as follows:

```
create actor (state1, state2, ..., staten)
actor msg1:arg1 msg2:arg2 ... msgn:argn →
continuation
```

Figure 5.5 gives the representation of an actor. The horizontal arrow represents its life, the broken line the sending of messages and the dotted lines the creation of other actors.

When an actor receives a message the patterns in its filter are compared with that message, the pattern matching the message is selected and the corresponding action is initiated; if no match is found the message is sent on to the actor's proxy if there is one; if not an error is signalled.

In programming with actors we have to forget all previous knowledge of programming and learn new methods designed specifically for parallelism. Take for example the factorial, which as everyone knows can be written as a recursive function; this would be written in terms of actors as follows.

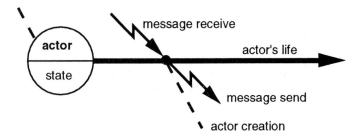

Figure 5.5 Representation of an actor.

```
actor           factorial
filter
  fact: 0 → r  [r send: 1].
  fact: i → r  [cont ← create mult(i,r).
               self fact: (i - 1) → cont].
actor           mult
state           val rec
filter
  send: v  [rec send: (v*val)].
```

The actor `factorial` has two message patterns, both concerning the message `fact:` and both with a continuation. The first recognizes `fact:` only when its argument is zero, the second recognizes the other messages `fact:`. This actor uses another, `mult`, to enable it to perform the computation. `mult`'s state consists of an integar `val` and an actor `rec`. When `mult` receives the message `send:` it passes `send:` to `rec` with argument the product of `val` and the value received – that is, it performs a multiplication and transmits the result to an actor which was specified when `mult` was created.

When the actor `factorial` receives a message asking it to compute the factorial of an integer `i` and to send the result to the continuation `r` it first creates an actor `mult`, which will multiply `i` by the value that will be sent to it, and send the result to `r`. Next, `factorial` sends itself a message asking itself to compute the factorial of `i-1` and to send the result to the actor `mult` which it has just created; thus `mult` will multiply the factorial of `i-1` by `i`, producing the result expected.

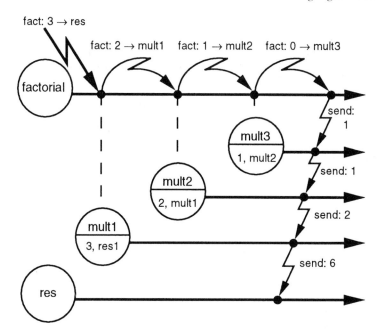

Figure 5.6 Computation of a factorial (3!).

When `factorial` has to compute the factorial of 0 it sends 1 directly to the continuation of the message, ending the computation and avoiding sending an unending sequence of `factorial` messages to itself.

Figure 5.6 shows the computation of a single factorial. A set $mult_i$ of actors is created, one for each step in the computation, each of which is inactive until it receives the message `send:`. The sequential computation (of 3!) is started by `factorial` sending the message `send:` to $mult_3$.

Thus the actor model forces us to transform a recursion into a set of actors that represents the progress of the computation. In this example the computation is strictly sequential, but the actor `factorial` is capable of computing several factorials simultaneously. Figure 5.7 shows how this can be done: here it receives two messages `fact:` and the two corresponding computations are interlaced; the messages provide sufficient

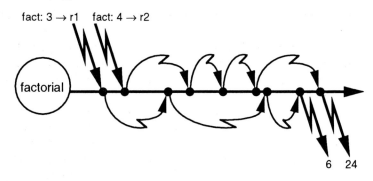

Figure 5.7 Simultaneous computation of several factorials.

information, in the form of continuations, to ensure that there is
no confusion.

Other programming techniques are available with the actor
model, of which we shall discuss only that of joint continuations;
we give an example of this later.

5.2.2   Message passing

Actor languages cast a new light on the sending of messages in
object-oriented languages. It is in fact only in actor languages
that the term 'message passing' is strictly correct, since in other
languages what is really involved is the invoking of procedures
or functions.

The asynchronous mode of communication that we have used
up to the present is not the only one available in actor languages;
ABCL/1, for example, has two others. One of these, **synchronous
communication**, corresponds to the sending of a message and
waiting for a response; here the continuation is necessarily the
sender, which is blocked until it receives the response. The other
mode, **anticipated communication**, enables this last constraint to
be lifted: the sender can continue with other activities while
waiting for the response, and can question the receiver to find if
the response is available. Thus an actor can send messages and
collect the responses as and when it needs them.

In addition, ABCL/1 offers two modes for transmission of
messages: the standard mode, in which the messages are simply

put into the receiver's mailbox, and an express mode. In the latter the actor is interrupted when the message arrives and deals with it immediately unless it is already dealing with a previously received express message; if it is, the message is put into a special 'express' mailbox which is always dealt with before the standard box.

Express messages enable interrupts to be generated. Suppose an actor represents an array and there is a message that enables the array to be searched for a specified element; on receiving such a message the actor can decide to share the task among a number of other actors, each of which will search independently a different part of the array. As soon as any one of these actors has found the required element there is no need for any of the others to continue searching, and the main actor can interrupt them by sending an express message. If this were not possible each actor would have to break its search into small steps, sending messages to itself so that the interrupt message can be acted on.

These different types of communication and modes of message transmission are provided with the aim of simplifying programming with actors; but even with these aids this can prove disconcerting.

5.2.3 Objects and actors

An obvious question is, to what extent are actor languages object-oriented languages? An actor is an object in the sense that it has a state and a form of behaviour, but differs from an object in that it is active and more like a process. This difference is seen clearly in the example of the factorial: the actor is an object which computes a factorial, whilst a traditional object-oriented language would see the factorial as a message sent to a number. Thus an actor is able to represent a behaviour or a computation, which is something an object cannot do. But an actor can also represent a state together with the associated methods, just as an object can, and such actors can be made to create computational actors so as to be able to respond to a message. This is illustrated by the following example.

The example concerns the Towers of Hanoi game and the solution of the problem associated with this, for which we shall need to use lists as in Lisp. A list is written enclosed in braces; it can respond to the synchronous messages `append:` `head` and `tail`, which respectively append an object to the list, return the head of the list and return the tail. It can be scanned by the message `repeat:` which takes as argument a block with an argument. We denote synchronous messages by using the symbol '⏎' as continuation; these can return a value by using the operator '↑'.

The actor `Tower` will represent a tower, whose state is the stack of discs; whilst `Hanoi` will represent the game as a whole.

```
actor   Tower
state   stack top
filter
   Push: x  [stack at: top put: x ⏎.
             top ← top + 1].
            [top ← top - 1].
   Pop      [top ← top - 1].
   Top      [↑stack at: top ⏎].
```

The actor `Tower` is a stack. We have not included a test to compare the size of the object to be added with that of the current front; this is not needed here, because the program for solving the problem will incorporate it into the rules of the game. `Top` is a synchronous message which returns the object at the stack front. We assume that the actor that represents the stack understands the access messages `at:` and `at:put:`. An object is put on the stack (`Push:`) by means of a synchronous message.

```
actor   Hanoi
state   left right centre nd
filter
   Initialize
      [(1 to nd) repeat [:i | left Push: (nd - 1)]].
   move: dep to: arr
      [arr Push: (dep Front ⏎). dep Pop].
   Play
      [hg ← create HanoiGame (self).
       hg move: nd from: left to: right
       by: centre tag: 1 → hg].
```

The actor `Hanoi` represents the game. `Initialize` puts nd discs on the left-hand tower, in order of decreasing size. `move:to:` transfers a disc from the tower given as the first argument to that given as the second; it sends the synchronous message `Top` to the departure tower, puts the value returned on the arrival tower and removes the discs from the departure tower. `Play` starts the process of solving the problem by creating an actor `HanoiGame` for this purpose: the sequential recursive algorithm for this is:

```
-- move n discs from the tower
-- dep to the tower arr using
-- the intermediate tower inter

procedure Hanoi(n:integer; dep, arr, inter:
    tower) {
  if n ≠ 0 then {
    Hanoi (n - 1, dep, inter, arr);
    MoveDisc (dep, arr);
    Hanoi (n - 1, inter, arr, dep);
  }
```

With actors, the difficulty here is to achieve a parallel solution that will generate an ordered list of disc movements. Using the same technique as for computing the factorial, and a new technique called **joint continuation**, we are going to create actors that represent the different steps in the computation, that is, the successive subsequences of disc movements.

```
actor  HanoiGame
state  hanoi
filter
  move:1 from:D to:A by:M tag:t → cont
    [cont tag:t list:{D A}].
  move:n from:D to:A by:M tag:t → cont
    [c ← create Join(cont, t, {D, A}, 0].
    self move:n - 1 from:D to:M by:A
    tag:
      t*2 → c.
    self move:n - 1 from:D to:M by:D
    tag:
      t*2 + 1 → c.
  ].
```

```
tag:t list: listmove
[listmove repeat:
  [:d | hanoi move: (d head ↵)
     to: (d tail ↵) ↵]
].
```

When it receives the message `move:from:to:by:tag:` the
actor `HanoiGame` creates an actor `Join` for joining continuations
and sends two messages for solving the two subproblems. The
join actor is initialized with the middle move and the
continuation of `HanoiGame`. It waits for the two lists of moves,
joins them with the middle move and sends the result to the
continuation. Here is the structure of this actor:

```
actor  Join
state  cont t listmove wait
filter
  tag:t*2 list: left
    [listmove ← left append: listmove ↵.
     self send].
  tag:t*2 + 1 list: right
    [listmove ← listmove append: right ↵.
     self send].
send
  [wait ← wait+1.
   (wait  =  2)   ifTrue:   [cont   tag:t
     list:listmove]].
```

In order to combine correctly the lists of moves, the join actor
must be able to distinguish the two lists that it receives. For this,
the solution messages carry a label, `tag`, which acts as a
numerical identifier for each solution: the solution with label n
generates two solutions, with labels $2*n$ and $2*n+1$ respectively.
The join actor is initialized with the label of the solution for
which it has been created, and can therefore determine the origin
of the lists it receives and consequently can combine their moves.
The message `send` enables the final move to be sent to the
continuation when the two sublists have been received.

   The message `tag:list:` is sent by `HanoiGame` when it has
only a single disc to move, and by `Join` after it has combined
the lists with the middle move. It is received either by `Join`, in
which case it contains the sublists of moves, or by `HanoiGame`

itself when the game is finished – the value of the label then being of no further use. When `HanoiGame` receives the final solution it enumerates the list of disc movements and sends `move:to:`messages to `Hanoi`; these messages are sent synchronously so as to ensure that they are handled in the order in which they are sent – otherwise the whole process would be rendered useless.

Figure 5.8 shows the initialization of an actor `Hanoi` with 2 discs, and the corresponding solution.

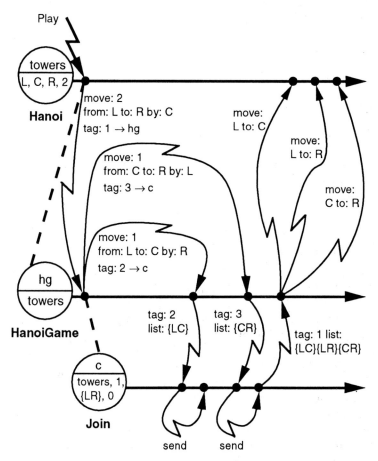

Figure 5.8 Solution of Towers of Hanoi.

```
towers ← create Hanoi (
   create Tower (create Array, 0),   -- left
   create Tower (create Array, 0),   -- middle
   create Tower (create Array, 0),   -- right
   2)
```

The amount of parallelism achieved is rather small; the actors Join and HanoiGame operate in parallel, but the bulk of the work is done by the latter. With n discs there would be a single HanoiGame actor and $2^{n-1}-1$ Join actors; the solution time increases exponentially with n, since HanoiGame sends itself 2^{n-1} messages which it treats sequentially.

More parallelism could be achieved by creating a HanoiGame actor at each step in the breakdown of the problem. There would then be $2*(n-1)$ of these and $2^{n-1}-1$ Join actors, and the solution time would be a linear function of n.

5.2.4   Conclusion

Programming with actor languages is not simple, but this is true for all parallel languages; the actor model is, however, easy to understand, and this is not true for all models of parallelism.

Actor languages are closer to prototype-based than to class-based languages: both use delegation, and creating actors is not very different from cloning. There are historical reasons for this resemblance. Most actor languages are contemporary with the first prototype-based languages and most have been developed on top of Lisp; consequently most are untyped, have no modularity mechanisms and use dynamic inheritance. Work on actor languages has focused primarily on the semantics of message passing, to the neglect of other aspects.

Prototype-based and actor languages diverge from the strict model of class-based languages; exploration of these contributes to the better understanding of programming with objects, and we can expect these studies to have a valuable influence on the more traditional object-oriented languages.

6

Programming with objects

This chapter describes some of the commonly used techniques of object-oriented programming, and gives a sketch of a general methodology. It ends with the full program for the Towers of Hanoi problem, which we have used as an example throughout the book. The methods given here can be used with both typed and untyped languages, but the example program is given in the language defined in Chapter 3; some of the points we make are therefore specific to typed languages.

In contrast to imperative and functional programming, object-oriented programming is centred on the data structures that are manipulated; consequently development of a program takes place in three phases, as follows:

1. identification of the classes;
2. definition of the protocol for each class, that is, specification of its public methods (the methods visible from outside the class);
3. definition of the fields and implementation of the method bodies; possibly, definition of private methods (visible only from within the class).

Correct identification of the classes, correct use of inheritance and proper definition of protocols are critically important for creating reusable classes. It is important also to experiment with object-oriented programming before using it on a serious problem, so as to get a good feeling for both its subtleties and its limitations.

6.1 IDENTIFYING THE CLASSES

This may seem easy but in fact is demanding. Too many classes will entail an over-complex functionality, too few will necessitate over-complex relations between the classes; only experience will teach how to strike the right balance. Methods for designing object-oriented programs are still in their infancy; object-oriented design methods – not to be confused with the preceding – are more developed, but are not always well adapted to design of object-oriented systems: some, for example, take no account of inheritance. A good plan is to study the libraries of classes provided for the existing languages or available to these. The Smalltalk library in particular is very instructive; it includes the classes that together implement the operating system and also those for the programming environment and for the graphics system.

We shall distinguish several categories of classes, and whilst not exhaustive our list will give an idea of the variety of roles that a class can play in an application.

6.1.1   Categories of classes

Atomic. These represent autonomous objects, that is, objects whose state as seen from outside the class is independent of all other classes. Examples are geometrical classes (e.g. points, vectors) and graphical classes (e.g. rectangles, circles). The class of stacks is not atomic, since a stack can contain objects that can be accessed.

Composite. Instances of these are collections of components that are accessible from outside the class: 'accessible' means that some knowledge of the component can be gained, or some action performed, even if some limitation is imposed. For example, the access allowed may be simply to read a value, or to address a component only through the intermediary of a symbolic name such as an index or a character string. The Towers of Hanoi form a composite class; the example given later in this chapter will show that a tower has to be accessed symbolically, by means of a variable of numerical type.

Container. This is a particular case of the composite class. An instance will contain a collection of objects and will provide methods for adding to, removing from and searching the collection. Also it may, and often will, provide methods for enumerating the objects, often through the intermediary of an active class or an iterator – these are defined below. A typical example is the class of stacks.

Active. These classes represent processes rather than states. In Smalltalk the active classes are the blocks, which we used in Chapter 4 to define the control structure. Another example is provided by the class of **iterators**: an interator is an object that enables us to enumerate the components of another object, which latter is usually a container. One method of the iterator returns the next object after the one enumerated. The iterator stores the current state of the enumeration, thus making it possible for several iterators to act simultaneously on the same object. We give an example of an iterator later in this section.

Abstract. Such classes are not intended for instantiation, but rather to serve as the root for a hierarchy of subclasses. In general, they have no fields; their methods must be redefined for each derived class or must call methods which must themselves be redefined.

An abstract class can be used to define a general protocol that makes no assumptions concerning the implementation of derived classes. A good way to ensure that a set of classes can be extended is to insert abstract classes at strategic points in the inheritance tree.

An example is the abstract class `Collection`, described below. This has the methods of addition and withdrawal of elements, and of searching for a given element; these must be virtual methods if the language being used requires explicit declaration of dynamic binding, as does C++. The derived classes, `Set`, `List`, `File`, etc., must redefine these methods so as to be appropriate to the implementation:

```
Collection = class {
  methods
    procedure Add (Object);
    procedure Withdraw (Object);
    function Search (Object): boolean;
    function Next (Object): Object;
}
```

An abstract class can contain methods whose bodies are defined within the class, such as the method `AddIfAbsent`:

```
procedure AddIfAbsent (o: Object) {
  if not Search (o) then Add (o);
}
```

By imposing a protocol on the derived classes an abstract class enables the classes to be made more homogeneous. Thus Collection here allows the single name Add to be used with both Set and List, instead of Add for the first and Insert for the second.

An abstract class can be used to define general classes, and so can compensate for any absence of genericity. If A is an abstract class and C an arbitrary class, then declaration in C of fields or method arguments of class A makes it possible to use a wider range of objects with C than if a concrete class had been used. For example, if we wished to define a general class Iterator, starting with the class Collection defined above, then unless we could use an abstract class we should have to redefine the iterator class for every container class.

```
Iterator = class {
  fields
    coll: Collection;
    current: Object;
  methods
    procedure Initialize (c: Collection) {
      c:= coll;
      current:= coll.Next (NULL);
    }
    function Next ( ): Object {
      o: Object;
      o: current;
      if o ≠ NULL
      then current:= coll.Next (current);
      return o;
    }
}
```

Here we have assumed that Collection.Next(NULL) returns the first object of the collection, and that Collection.Next(o) returns NULL when o is the last element. NULL is a special object which serves to simplify the writing of the program text.

6.1.2 Inheritance or nesting?

The main problem in identifying classes lies in the choice of the inheritance tree. What has to be determined is whether or not a given class should inherit from some other, and if so, from which. Typed languages are more constraining here than untyped because the choice of the inheritance will determine how the instances of the class can be used. Thus in the example of the class Collection, above, if a class is defined that does not inherit from it but which defines the method Next, it will not be possible to apply the class Iterator to the objects of this latter class. That would be possible with an untyped language, for then all that Iterator requires of the iterated object is that it should respond to the message Next. It follows that the choice of the inheritance tree will be more difficult with a typed object-oriented language, and that greater consequences will follow from whatever choice is made.

Inheritance is a powerful mechanism, in the sense that it can be used in different contexts. It is used most frequently for specialization and enrichment, as illustrated in the preceding chapters by having the class Tower inherit from Stack, a tower being a special kind of stack. At the same time we have taken care not to inherit Stack from some hypothetical class Array, preferring to put the array within the stack.

Inheritance leads to an ordering of the classes; this encourages its use when the classes have compatible protocols – that is, when the protocol of one is included in that of another – and discourages this when only the structures are compatible, that is, when the structure of one is a subset of that of the other. It is protocol compatibility that allows inheritance to be used not only for specialization (in the case when the inclusion is actual equality) but also for enrichment: a tower has the same protocol as a stack – push, pop, top – whilst that of an array allows access to be made to any element, which is incompatible with the stack protocol.

The semantics of inheritance is such that not only the protocol but also the structure of a derived class must be compatible with that of the base class, since the fields are inherited. This can give rise to problems: a hierarchy chosen solely on the basis of compatibility of protocols can be invalidated at a later stage by incompatibility of structures. The difficulty can generally be avoided by creating abstract classes, of which the classes with incompatible structures are subclasses.

Consider for example the class Polygon, with the methods draw, rotate and translate. The class Rectangle, representing rectangles whose sides are horizontal and vertical respectively, has a protocol that is compatible with that of Polygon and could therefore inherit from Polygon. However, for reasons of efficiency we might want to represent a rectangle by a pair of diagonally opposite points, whereas a polygon requires a list of consecutive points, and this would make inheritance impossible. The solution would be to introduce an abstract class, Shape say, as follows.

```
Shape = class {
  methods
    procedure Draw (w: Window);
    procedure Rotate (centre: Point; angle: real);
    procedure Translate: (v: Vector);
}

Polygon = class Shape {
  fields
    points: List [Point];
  methods
    (as Shape)
}

Rectangle = class Shape {
  fields
    p1, p2: Point;
  methods
    (as Shape)

}
```

The same problem could arise in defining a class Square; logically, this should inherit from Rectangle, but if we wanted to represent a square by a point and a length it would be necessary to define a class Quadrilateral, a subclass of Shape, of which Rectangle and Square were in turn subclasses. This is an undesirable burdening of the inheritance hierarchy.

Attempts to use inheritance for purposes other than specialization or enrichment generally result in an unsatisfactory solution or even in outright failure. Using inheritance between classes with compatible structures but incompatible protocols, for example between `Array` and `Stack`, can be acceptable if the language allows the inheritance relation to be hidden from the point of view of inclusion of types, as is the case, for example, in C++ with its private inheritance; otherwise it is better to abandon this use, even at the cost of some burdening of the programming.

6.1.3 Multiple inheritance

This is a source of many problems. Repeated inheritance can lead to conflicts of names, as we have already mentioned; multiple inheritance can give rise also to semantic and methodological problems. With our treatment of protocol compatibility we can decide that multiple inheritance is justified if the protocol of the subclass is compatible with that of each of its superclasses. Conflicts can arise if some part of the protocol for the subclass is included in the protocols of more than one of the superclasses: an example was given in Chapter 3, with the method `Write` in the class `TowerGM` inheriting from both `Tower` and `Window`. In such a case it is essential to redefine in the subclass that part of the protocol that is the source of the conflict; if multiple inheritance is justified at all, the redefined protocol must make reference to the superclass protocols.

Like simple inheritance, multiple inheritance enforces inheritance of structure from the parent classes, and this raises the problem encountered in repeated inheritance: if the same field in a particular class is inherited by two or more different routes, should this field be replicated? Although the languages provide a variety of control mechanisms, as we have seen, there is a great risk here of the hierarchy of the classes being made unusable, and it is safer not to use multiple inheritance. There is however one situation in which repeated inheritance can be used safely, without risk of conflict of structures: this is when the class that is inherited by several routes is an abstract class without fields.

Thus multiple inheritance can be used when it will not lead to protocol conflicts and the inherited classes have no common ancestor containing fields. It will then give an **agglomerated** class (also called **mix-in**). This approximates to a composite class made up of one field from each inherited class; the difference is that any instance of an agglomerated class is compatible in type with each of the inherited classes. Each inherited class constitutes a different facet of the agglomerated class and the conditions imposed ensure the independence of these facets. Inheritance polymorphism for agglomerated classes corresponds to using one facet of the class.

The similarity between agglomeration and composition indicates that the latter can be used in place of the former when multiple inheritance is to be avoided for any of the reasons given above. The consequence is that neither the facets nor the programming features associated with these are available, but the resulting set of classes is easier to handle.

Whilst composition can replace multiple inheritance, the reverse is not true: the protocol, not the structure, determines the inheritance. It is not true that because an automobile consists of an engine, a body and four wheels that the class `Automobile` must inherit from `Engine`, from `Body` and four times from `Wheel`.

6.2   DEFINING THE METHODS

We have just seen how the classes and the inheritance tree are defined; in particular, it will have become clear that the concept of protocol is crucial in determining inheritance. We now give the elements that are needed to help define the protocols, that is, the public methods of the classes; and as with the classes, we give a classification of these methods.

Access methods enable us to obtain information about the content of an object, and to modify its state, without producing any side effects. An access can simply return the value of a field, assign a value, or perform a computation which uses or modifies the values of an object's fields. In the latter case we call it a **computational** rather than an access method. Most languages of the Smalltalk family generate automatically, for each field, an access method for reading and another for writing: this acts against encapsulation, since it makes every field freely available to all users.

Construction methods enable us to set up relations between objects. Objects often need to have knowledge of each other so as to be able to exchange messages, and this knowledge must be kept up to date. Determining the right construction methods is a difficult task, since the relations between objects are often complex.

To take an example, a window must 'know' what graphics objects it contains, and these objects must know in which window they are. Two problems arise: where to put the construction method and how to establish the relation, which in this case will be bidirectional. The method Add could be either in the class of windows or in the class of graphics objects – or we could decide to put it in both. In any case, the method of one of the classes must call a method in the other, in order to establish the reciprocal relationship, as in the following:

```
procedure Window. Add (og: OGraphic) {
    ...                     -- add og to the window
    og.AddedIn (me);   -- inform og
}
```

Here the classes Window and OGraphic are in a special relation with each other. If some other class were to call OGraphic.AddedIn directly this would be contrary to the reciprocal nature of the relation and would lead to an error state of the system; it must therefore be made impossible for any class other than Window to make this call, and this can be done by means of mechanisms for controlling visibility, such as the friends of C++ or the export lists of Eiffel.

Control methods initiate a computation in which several objects take part, using the graph of objects that results from the application of the construction methods. A control method does not itself perform any computation but determines which objects should be involved and sends them all or part of the computation: for example, displaying the contents of a window is a control method that requires each of the objects in the window to be redrawn.

As with construction methods, control methods often need to be able to call special methods that are not accessible to other users of the objects in question. The example below concerns redisplaying the contents of a window; the method needs to call the private method InitDraw for the window so as to set up the environment necessary for redrawing the objects.

```
procedure Window.Redraw ( ) {
  InitDraw ( );   -- sets up the environment
  for each graphics o object do -
    o.Redraw ( );
}
procedure OGraphic.Redraw ( ) {
  . . .
}
```

Since the methods for drawing graphics objects must be visible only to the classes that are able to put this environment in place before calling them, OGraphic.Redraw must be visible only to Window.

Class methods are those methods that are global to a class; they play the role of global procedures and functions but have the advantage of obeying the same visibility rules as apply to ordinary methods. If the language has metaclasses then the class methods are defined in these, otherwise a special mechanism is provided for declaring class fields and class methods. Class methods are used for accessing the class fields so as to control the set of instances; a use that we have already seen is to give a unique number to these instances, another is to control the kind of trace messages issued by the methods, and so provide an aid to development.

6.2.1 Defining the visibility of the methods

The above examples have shown the importance of visibility of methods for the safety of the program. Untyped languages in general provide no control for this: thanks to the access methods that are created automatically, every method, and indeed every field, is visible from every class. With typed languages, in contrast, domains of visibility can be defined. This difference is reflected in the different ways in which the two families are used. A typed language is the better choice when what is wanted is strong encapsulation, to give greater program safety by allowing as many static checks as possible to be made. An untyped language is more likely to be used for prototyping, when the need is for unrestricted access to the objects so as to aid incremental development. Determining the right visibility domain for each method is often a difficult task, even when sophisticated control methods are available, as in Eiffel. This is especially the case if the class is intended to be reusable, for then the interface will in general need to be modified for each different use, most often by making more methods visible. The domains needed are

1. private, visible only to the class
2. visible to subclasses
3. visible to a privileged class
4. public, visible to all classes.

Of these, the domain for a privileged class is the most difficult to define without over-proliferating the privileged classes of any given class. In a well-designed system the classes will work in groups, and the privileged classes for any class are the other classes in its group; this reduces the interdependencies between classes and makes their reuse easier.

6.2.2 Double dispatching

In object-oriented languages the semantics of message sending is a matter of determining the method to be invoked, according to the class of the receiver. It often happens, however, that the receiver alone does not suffice to determine the right method, since this can depend also on the classes of the parameters in the message. In typed languages inheritance polymorphism enables objects belonging to a subclass of the class declared for the formal parameters to be passed as actual parameters; in untyped languages, obviously, the classes of the parameters play no part.

In both cases the problem is solved by means of the technique of double dispatching, illustrated by the following example. `Display` and `OGraphic` are abstract classes which provide methods for representing graphics objects on peripherals. The choice of method in any particular case depends on the class of both the peripheral and the object; with the peripheral classes

`Window` and `Printer` the double dispatching method is implemented as follows.

```
Display = class {
  methods
    procedure Draw(o: OGraphic);
}
Window = class Display {
  methods
    procedure Draw(o: OGraphic) {
      o.DisplayWindow(me);
    }
}
Printer = class Display {
  methods
    procedure Draw(o:OGraphic) {
      o.DisplayPrinter(me);
    }
}
```

The method `Draw` is redefined in each derived class and calls a method of `OGraphic`, the name of which specifies the sender subclass; this is the first stage of the double dispatching. The second stage takes place in the subclasses of `OGraphic`: the method for producing the display is redefined for each peripheral, as follows.

```
OGraphic = class {
  methods
    procedure DisplayWindow(disp:Window)
    procedure DisplayPrinter(disp:Printer);
}
Rectangle = class OGraphic {
  ...
  methods
    procedure DisplayWindow(disp:Window) {
      ... -- draw a rectangle on the screen
    }
    procedure DisplayPrinter(disp:Printer) {
      ... -- draw a rectangle on the printer
    }
}
```

```
Circle = class OGraphic {
  ...
  methods
    procedure DisplayWindow(disp:Window) {
      ... -- draw a circle on the screen
    }
    procedure DisplayPrinter(disp:Printer) {
      ... -- draw a circle on the printer
    }
}
```

The mechanism is shown in Figure 6.1. The first stage of the dispatching takes place in the subclasses of Display, the second in those of OGraphic; specifying a graphics object together with the peripheral on which to display it determines which display method from OGraphic is called.

If we add a subclass to Display we must define the method Draw for this subclass; we must also add the corresponding display method to OGraphic and an implementation of the method to each of its subclasses. If we add a subclass to OGraphic we must implement in this the display methods for every peripheral. It is important to note that a new class of graphics objects can be added without the need to modify the display classes, but that the inverse is not true; this can help to decide how the double dispatch should be implemented.

If there are n and p subclasses of Display and OGraphic respectively, n methods must be implemented in each of p subclasses, a total of n*p implementations, which is not

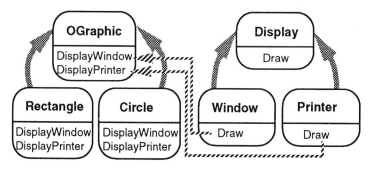

Figure 6.1 Double dispatching.

surprising, since the method for producing the display must depend on both the display device and the object to be displayed; and in addition a dispatch method for each subclass must be added to `Display`, a further n methods. This cost is acceptable, however, in view of the services that double dispatching provides.

If a typed language that allows overloading (methods with the same name but different parameter lists) is used, the different dispatching methods can all have the same name, which in this case would be `Display`.

6.3   REUSING THE CLASSES

The possibility of reusing classes is undoubtedly one of the important advantages of object-oriented languages, but defining reusable classes can be difficult. The need arises when we wish to design a library, that is, a set of classes that provides some particular service. Such a library will in general contain classes to be used as they are and others from which further classes are expected to be derived, giving reuse by inheritance. Genericity provides a powerful means for reuse, but since this is not a feature of all languages we shall not consider it here.

When we start to design a library we shall have formed some idea of the type of reuse that we expect; but it is usually found that the reuse made in practice is not what was expected: the users' needs may turn out not to correspond exactly with the services offered by the library, the method of reuse provided is not well adapted to the application, or the users may simply fail to use the method well. The greater the extent to which a library of classes can be used in ways that were not foreseen, the more powerful it is; we shall consider some techniques that can help to attain such a goal.

Some classes can be expected to be reused directly, but most reuse will be by means of inheritance; this is especially true for abstract classes. Reuse by inheritance consists of redefining the methods of the base class and adding new methods and new fields, and the redefinition is the source of most of the problems. The base class must specify which methods *must* be redefined, which methods *may* and which *must not*: these three types depend on the protocol of the base class, and the base class cannot be reused correctly without a knowledge of this. A policy that is particularly safe is to allow only private methods to be redefined. The following is an example:

```
AbstractStack = class {
  private methods
     procedure Add(o: Object);    -- to be redefined
     procedure Remove( );         -- to be redefined
     function IsEmpty( )
     boolean;                     -- to be redefined
     function Last: Object;       -- to be redefined
     procedure StackEmpty( );     -- to be redefined
  methods                         -- public methods
     procedure Push(o: Object) {
       Add(o);
     }
     procedure Pop( ) {
       if not IsEmpty( ) then Remove( );
     }
     function Top: Object {
       if not IsEmpty( )
          then return Last( )
          else { StackEmpty( ); return NULL; }
     }
}
```

Whilst this example is so simple as to be rather unrealistic it does show that forbidding redefinition of public methods prevents the creation of a subclass that contravenes the semantics of a stack. Any attempt to access the top of a stack that is empty constitutes an error, and the method `StackEmpty` enables us to redefine the way in which such an error is signalled or handled.

In general, the public protocol ensures that the semantics of the class is respected, whilst the private protocol defines atomic operations that are to be redefined in each subclass. This does not prevent a method of the public protocol from being redefined in a subclass, should the need arise, as might be desirable in the interests of efficiency.

6.3.1   Dependent classes

The commonest use of composite or agglomerated classes is in creating classes that are intended to work together as a set; reuse of such classes must be done by deriving them in parallel, and this presents special problems. In our previous example concerning Window and OGraphic (section 6.2.2), a window contains a list of objects to be displayed, and a graphic object contains the window in which it is to be displayed. The usual aim of parallel derivation is to define new classes which, like their base classes, will work as a team. Suppose now that we want to define new classes Window3D and OGraphic3D that will display objects in three dimensions:

```
Window3D = class Window {
  public methods
    procedure Add(o: OGraphic);    -- inherited
}
OGraphic3D = class OGraphic {
  private methods
    procedure AddIn(w: Window);    -- inherited
}
```

A three-dimensional window can contain only three-dimensional objects, but this, unfortunately, is not expressed in the inherited methods, since the procedure Window.Add can take any object as a parameter and OGraphic.AddIn can take any window as argument.

In untyped languages it is easy to check the actual class of an object, as we showed in Chapter 4 for the case of HStack; but this is not so in typed languages, and in the present example we should need to redefine the method Add to take a parameter of type OGraphic3D.

Some languages, Eiffel in particular, allow a method to be redefined in a subclass with parameters whose types are included in those of the corresponding parameters in the base class. Unfortunately, the type cannot then be checked statically, and consequently Eiffel has to be classed as a weakly typed language. This is illustrated by the following example.

```
U = class {
  procedure g( );
}
A = class {
  procedure f(p: U) {
  }
}

V = class {
  procedure h( );
}
B = class {
  procedure f(p: V){
  }
}

a: A; b: B; u: U;
a = b;      -- inclusive polymorphism
a.f(u);     -- dynamic binding calls B.f;
```

Here the method f is redefined in the class B with a parameter that belongs to a subclass of B declared for A. f; the call a. f (u) is correct so far as static typing is concerned. At run time a contains an object of class B and therefore, because of the dynamic binding, B. f will be called. But B. f expects a parameter of type V, whilst what is passed is of type U, so an error should be signalled. To prevent this the compiler must generate code that will check the actual types of the objects at run time, making the language weakly-typed.

With languages that do not provide such a mechanism the only certain way to deal with the problem is to provide a means for ascertaining and testing the class of an object; and this comes down to defining objects which represent classes, such as the metaclasses of the object-oriented languages of the Smalltalk family.

Whatever the language, if parallel derivation is used then all idea of static typing must be given up; the consequence is that much greater care must be taken in the design of the system to minimize the number of situations in which dynamic control of types is necessary.

6.4 EXAMPLE: THE TOWERS OF HANOI

We now give the complete program for the Towers of Hanoi game. The starting point is the class `Tower` defined in Chapter 3; using this, we define the class `Hanoi`, representing the game, as follows:

```
TowerPos = (left, centre, right);
Hanoi = class {
  fields
    towers: array[TowerPos] of Tower;
  methods
    procedure Build( );
    procedure Initialize(n: integer);
    procedure Move(from, to: TowerPos);
    procedure Play(from, to, by: TowerPos;
    n: integer);
}
```

The type `TowerPos` serves to identify the three towers. `Hanoi` is a composite class allowing controlled access to its components. The bodies of the methods are as follows:

```
procedure Hanoi.Build( ) {
  towers[left]:= allocate(Tower);
  towers[centre]:= allocate (Tower);
  towers[right]:= allocate (Tower);
}

procedure Hanoi.Initialize(n: integer) {
  towers[left].Initialize(n);
  towers[centre].Clear( )
  towers[right].Clear( );
}

procedure Hanoi.Move(from, to: TowerPos) {
  d: integer;
  d:= towers[from].Top( );
  if towers[from].CanPush(d) then {
    towers[from].Pop( );
    towers[to].Push(d);
  } else
```

```
      error.Write("Move: impossible");
   }

   procedure Hanoi.Play(from, to, by: TowerPos;
   n: integer) {
     if n > 0 then {
       Play(from, by, to, n - 1);
       Move(from, to);
       output.Write(from, " → ", to);
       Play(by, to, from, n - 1);
     }
   }
```

error and output are global objects which enable us to display messages on the screen; allocate creates an object dynamically, similar to new in Pascal.

We could use the above as follows:

```
hanoi: Hanoi;
hanoi.Build();
hanoi.Initialize(4);
hanoi.Move(left, centre);
hanoi.Move(left, right);
hanoi.Move(right, centre);
   → play: move impossible
```

The automatic solution is as follows:

```
hanoi.Initialize(2);
hanoi.Play( );
   left   → centre;
   left   → right;
   centre → right;
```

6.4.1 Graphical Towers of Hanoi

We now show how we can use the class TowerG of Chapter 3 to define a class HanoiG that will represent the Towers of Hanoi game graphically. All that is necessary is to redefine the method Build so that we can allocate graphical instead of ordinary towers; since this will require a screen window for the display we shall have to add a suitable field in defining the new class.

```
HanoiG = class Hanoi {
  fields
    w: Window;
  private methods
    procedure BuildTower(t:  TowerPos;  x,  y:
    integer);
  methods
    procedure Build( );
}

procedure HanoiG.BuildTower(t: TowerPos; x, y:
integer) {
  towers[t] := allocate(TowerG);
  Tower[t].Place(w, x, y);
}

procedure HanoiG.Build( ) {
  w := allocate(Window);
  BuildTower(left, 10, 100);
  BuildTower(centre, 50, 100);
  BuildTower(right, 90, 100);
}
```

The method BuildTower is auxiliary to Build and therefore must be private.

The example already given for the class Hanoi applies equally for the class HanoiG. The display, however, will not show the movements of the discs; if we wish to show these – to animate the display, in fact – we must redefine the method Move:

```
procedure HanoiG.Move(from, to: TowerPos) {
  Hanoi.Move(from, to);
  ...                        -- show disc movements
}
```

But this is not very satisfactory, because if a proposed move is found to be invalid Hanoi.Move will issue an error message and the movement should not be shown. The only way to check the validity of a proposed move in HanoiG.Move would be to repeat the code of Hanoi.Move, and this would make the derived class HanoiG dependent on the implementation of Hanoi.

A better course is to modify the class Hanoi so as to make it more flexible from the point of view of reuse, as we did in section 6.3 for the class AbstractStack. For this we define a private method Shift to be called after Move when the proposed move is legal:

```
Hanoi = class {
  ...
  private methods
    ...
    procedure  Shift(d:  integer;  from,  to:
    TowerPos);
  methods
    procedure Move(from, to: TowerPos);
    ...
}

procedure Hanoi.Move(from, to: TowerPos) {
  d: integer;
  d:= towers[from].Top( );
  if towers[to].Push(d) then {
    towers[from].Pop();
    towers[to].Push(d);
    Shift(d, from, to);          -- signal the move
  } else
    error.Write("Move: move impossible");
}

procedure  Hanoi.Shift(d:  integer;  from,  to:
TowerPos) {
  -- default procedure, does nothing
}
```

The class HanoiG then becomes

```
HanoiG = class Hanoi {
  fields
    w: Window
  private methods
    procedure  BuildTower(t;  TowerPos;  x,  y:
    integer);
    procedure  Shift(d:  integer;  from,to:
    TowerPos);
  methods
    procedure Build(t);
```

```
procedure HanoiG.Shift(d: integer; from, to:
TowerPos) {
    -- animation to show disc movements
    ...
}
```

It is now not necessary to redefine Move. Extension of the base class Hanoi has been made possible by the addition of the private method Shift which informs the derived classes of any significant change of state. The fact that this did not become obvious until the solution by redefinition had been tried shows that when writing reusable classes it is important to know in what contexts they will be reused.

6.5 CONCLUSION

This chapter will have shown something of both the possibilities and the limitations of object-oriented languages; relative to other languages, these favour modularity and reuse but nevertheless do not provide complete solutions to the problems associated with these features.

The examples of application development that we have given will show that the use of classes can help in controlling the development of large systems, provided that great care has been taken in specifying the classes and that the requirements of the object-oriented model have been taken fully into consideration. In general, an object-oriented language is a powerful tool, but it is not a universal panacea: a problem is never solved by simply casting it in terms of objects.

Bibliography

GENERAL REFERENCES

Proc. ECOOP (European Conference on Object-Oriented Programming. *Lecture Notes in Computer Science*, Springer Verlag Vols.276 (1987), 322 (1988), 512 (1991).

Proc. OOPSLA (Object-Oriented Programming, Systems, Languages and Applications). *Special Issue SIGPLAN Notices*, ACM Vols. 21 no.11 (1986), 22 no.12 (1987), 23 no.11 (1988), 24 no.10 (1989), 25 no.10 (1991).

G. Agha (1986) *Actors: a Model of Concurrent Computation in Distributed Systems*. MIT Press, Cambridge (Mass.).

B.J. Cox (1986) *Object-Oriented Programming: an Evolutionary Approach*. Addison-Wesley, Reading (Mass.).

J. Ferber (1990) *Conception et Programmation par Objets*. Collection Techniques de Pointe. Hermès, Paris.

G. Masini, A. Napoli, D. Colnet, D. Léonard and K. Tombre (1989) *Les Langages à Objets*. InterEditions, Paris.

B. Meyer (1989) *Conception et Programmation par Objets*. InterEditions Paris.

B. Shriver and P. Wegner (eds.) (1987) *Research Directions in Object-Oriented Programming*. MIT Press Cambridge (Mass.).

D. Tsichritzis (ed.) Centre Universitaire d'Informatique, Université de Genève. *Objects and Things, 1987. Active Object Environments, 1988. Object Management, 1990. Object Composition* (1991).

A. Yonezawa and M. Tokoro (eds.) (1987) *Object-Oriented Concurrent Programming*. MIT Press, Cambridge (Mass.).

PARTICULAR TOPICS

Here and in the next section references in square brackets are to works cited above.

G. Agha & C.E. Hewitt. Actors: a Conceptual Foundation for Concurrent Object-Oriented Programming. In [Shriver & Wegner, 1987] pp.49–74.

G. Agha & C.E. Hewitt. Concurrent Programming Using Actors. In [Yonezawa & Tokoro 1987] pp.37–53.

P. Cointe (1985) *Implémentation et Interprétation des Langages Orientés Objets. Applications aux Langages Smalltalk, Objvlisp et Formes.* Doctoral Thesis, Université de Paris VII, LITP 85.55.

L. Cardelli and P. Wegner (1985) On Understanding Types, Data Abstraction and Polymorphism. *ACM Computing Surveys*, Vol.17, no.4, pp.471–522.

W.R. Cook, W.L. Hill and P. Canning (1990) Inheritance is not Subtyping. Proc. *Principles of Programming Languages*, ACM pp.125–135.

S. Danforth and C. Tomlinson (1988) Type Theories and Object-Oriented Programming. *ACM Computing Surveys*, Vol.20, no.1, pp.29–72.

R. Ducourneau and M. Habib (1989) La Multiplicité de l'Héritage dans les Langages à Objets. *Technique et Science Informatique*, Vol.8, no.1, pp.41–62.

K. Gorlen (1987) An Object-Oriented Class Library for C++ Programs. *Software Practice and Experience.* Vol.17, no.12, pp.899–922.

H. Lieberman. Using Prototypical Objects to Implement Shared Behaviour in Object-Oriented Systems. In [Proc. OOPSLA 1986] pp.214–223.

B. Meyer. Genericity versus Inheritance. In [Proc. OOPSLA 1986] pp.391–405.

D. Ungar, C. Chambers, B-W. Chang and U. Hölzle (1991) Organizing Programs without Classes. *International Journal of Lisp and Symbolic Computation.* Vol.4, no.3.

A. Yonezawa, E. Shibayama, T. Takada and Y. Honda. Modelling and Programming in Object-Oriented Concurrent Programming. In [Yonezawa & Tokoro 1987] pp.55–89.

OBJECT-ORIENTED PROGRAMMING LANGUAGES

Byte Special Issue: the Smalltalk-80 System. *Byte* Vol.6 no.8, 1981.

L. Cardelli, J. Donahue, L. Glassman, M. Jordan, B. Kalsow and G. Nelson (1989) *Modula-3 Report (revised).* Research Report 52, DEC Systems Research Centre, Palo Alto (Calif.).

P. Cointe. Metaclasses are First Class: the ObjVlisp Model. In [Proc. OOPSLA 1987] pp.1156–167.

O.J. Dahl and K. Nygaard (1986) Simula, An Algol-based Simulation Language. *Comm. of the ACM* Vol.9, no.9, pp.671–678.

L.G. De Michiel and R.P. Gabriel. The CommonLisp Object System: an Overview. In [Proc. ECOOP 1987] pp.201–220.

Eiffel, the Language. Interactive Software Engineering Inc. Goleta (Calif.) 1989.

M. Ellis and B. Stroustrup. (1893) *The Annotated C++ Reference Manual*. Addison-Wesley, Reading (Mass.).

A. Goldberg and D. Robson. (1983) *Smalltalk-80, the Language and its Implementation*. Addison-Wesley, Reading (Mass.).

S.E. Keene (1989) *Object-Oriented Programming in Common Lisp. A Programmer's Guide to CLOS*. Addison-Wesley, Reading (Mass.).

H. Lieberman. Concurrent Object-Oriented programming in Act1. In [Yonezawa & Tokoro 1987].

S. Lippman (1989) *A C++ Primer*. Addison-Wesley, Reading (Mass.).

D. Moon. Object-Oriented Programming with Flavors. In [Proc. OOPSLA 1986] pp.1–8.

K. Schmucker (1980) *Object-Oriented Programming for the Macintosh*. Hayden Book Company, Hasbrouck Heights (N. Jersey).

D. Ungar & R.B. Smith. Self: the Power of Simplicity. In [Proc. OOPSLA 1987] pp.227–242.

A. Yonezawa, J-P. Briot & E. Shibayama. Object-Oriented Concurrent Programming in ABCL/1. In [Proc. OOPSLA 1986] pp.252–68.

Author index

Index of Technical terms

The following entries are specialized technical terms, printed in the text as e.g. *AbstractStack*, and usually used as names of fields etc.

Index

138   *Index*